DO YOU LOVE ME?...
FEED MY SHEEP

Do You Love Me?...
Feed My Sheep

When Faith Meets Action

Rick Tunis

DESTINY IMAGE® PUBLISHERS, INC.

P.O. Box 310, Shippensburg, PA 17257-0310

"Speaking to the Purposes of God for This Generation and for the Generations to Come."

This book and all other Destiny Image, Revival Press, MercyPlace, Fresh Bread, Destiny Image Fiction, and Treasure House books are available at Christian bookstores and distributors worldwide.

For a U.S. bookstore nearest you, call 1-800-722-6774.

For more information on foreign distributors, call 717-532-3040.

Reach us on the Internet: www.destinyimage.com.

Trade Paper ISBN 13: 978-0-7684-3275-6
Hardcover ISBN 13: 978-0-7684-3505-4
Large Print ISBN 13: 978-0-7684-3506-1
Ebook ISBN 13: 978-0-7684-9090-9

For Worldwide Distribution, Printed in the U.S.A.

1 2 3 4 5 6 7 8 9 10 11 / 13 12 11 10

DEDICATION

To the love of my life, whom I can't wait to see come down the stairs every morning, Nancy Tunis.

You've been my wife, my best friend, and my biggest encourager for more than 27 years. You're my "Jersey Girl." Thank you for the tons of support you've given me through the years and for always being there when I needed you.

Contents

PART 2: FALLING AWAY FROM FOLLOWING

PART 3: COMING BACK TO JESUS

PART 4: BECOMING A SHEPHERD

INTRODUCTION

I said yes to Jesus when I was 16 years old, but over the years I traded in my spiritual usefulness for a life of compromise. God had not given up on me, but I couldn't be trusted with any assignments. It wasn't until I morphed into a more reliable and dependable disciple of Jesus Christ that the Lord began to call me and consistently use me for His purposes. Becoming usable to the Holy Spirit is what this book is about. When Jesus asked Peter in John's Gospel, "Do you love Me?... feed My sheep," Christ wanted Peter to recognize that if Peter truly loved Him, then Peter would live his life in such a way that he would be considered trustworthy for divine assignments (see John 21:17). Jesus was calling on Peter first to love Him and be trustworthy, and then to serve in his assigned calling.

It's like when I was about eight years old and my parents gave me a bow and arrow set for my birthday. It came complete with a target on a stand, and I couldn't wait to try it out! I unwrapped the package, ran out the storm door of our split-level home, and set up the target in front of the driveway. The arrow kept falling off the bow, but I finally got it on right and pulled hard. I let go of the arrow like I was Robin Hood, but instead of hitting the target, I had just shot the right front tire of my Dad's Buick. My parents weren't happy that I had shot the family car, but they didn't disown me, either. They didn't throw my clothes out of my bedroom window and into the front yard. But they did decide that I wasn't ready to be trusted with projectiles.

I think that this is also the way it is with our heavenly Father. When I asked Jesus to forgive me and come into my life, that was the beginning point of becoming a sheep in Christ's fold. God, like my parents, didn't disown me every time I did something stupid or wrong. But neither was He going to trust me with exciting divine assignments and the good works He had pre-planned for me to walk in. From personal experience, I have found that when things get turned around and a backsliding Christian like myself starts to respond to the Holy Spirit with consistent obedience, then He will put a fresh call on that person's life to help shepherd other sheep. *Do You Love Me?...Feed My Sheep* marries the concept of discipleship with usefulness and the "other" call of God. There's a world of work to be done out there and God's got big plans for you. He needs to get you to that level of faithfulness where He can say, "Hey I can use this one!" That's when the calling to work in His fields gets a little louder. That's when the assignments start to come. Let me take you on my journey going from failures to assignments; going from sheep to shepherd.

> *From personal experience, I have found that when things get turned around and a backsliding Christian like myself starts to respond to the Holy Spirit with consistent obedience, then He will put a fresh call on that person's life to help shepherd other sheep.*

Part One:

Becoming a Sheep
in Christ's Fold

Chapter 1

SHEEP NEED SHEPHERDS

Can you imagine wandering around aimlessly as a sheep without a shepherd? Once upon a time there was a wandering sheep named Cory. Cory was small and cute, and like her friends, she was lost but she didn't know she was lost. She was a very needy sheep because she lived her life without a caretaker or good pasture or clean water. There was little to no shelter around that would keep her warm from the cold, whipping winds, and she had no protection from the wolves, and she would often hear them howling at the moon. Day after day, some of her friends would suffer from a lack of food or they would just have a hollow feeling that there's nobody out there who cared about them. Corey's situation is a similar situation that many people find themselves in spiritually. There are billions of lost sheep in our world. In addition to the spiritually lost, there are countless believers who are barely holding on because they've been hurt, neglected, misled, or even abused. What's God's solution for the Corys of the world? Shepherds. Not just pastors, but anyone who is following Christ and has answered His call to help needy sheep.

The journey of every Christian's life should be all about becoming more and more useful to the Holy Spirit in order to bring salvation, healing, and spiritual health to the Corys who are in our families, our schools, our work, and even our churches. Once the Lord determines that you are usable, then He may call you to care for the well-being of someone across the street or around the world. God's plan for you is to take you from sheep to shepherd. It's about being usable for God's purposes, and His assignments are a whole lot more exciting and fulfilling than most people realize. My hope is that I can push, prod, inspire, and light a fire under every yo-yo Christian and every half-committed believer to wake up and get serious about their future calling! In this book, I've decided to use the stories of my own life to illustrate some of the pitfalls, dangers, snares, setbacks, and victories involved with getting a calling and becoming a shepherd of others. Each chapter will begin with a real-life illustration from my life and finish with a biblical teaching on discipleship and God's calling.

The journey of every Christian's life should be all about becoming more and more useful to the Holy Spirit in order to bring salvation, healing, and spiritual health to the Corys who are in our families, our schools, our work, and even our churches.

I am embarrassed to say that after getting saved during the Jesus movement of the '70s, I went from a state of usefulness and a sense of calling to a period in my life where my relationship with Jesus Christ became virtually nonexistent. After more than ten years of drifting, the great shepherd of my soul began to call me back. I didn't go after Him. He came after me. I'll explain this in greater detail later in the book. Let's just say that the Bible is dead-on when it describes people to be like straying sheep and in need of a shepherd. Jesus is our good shepherd and knows how to go after strays like me.

WHAT DOES THE BIBLE TELL US ABOUT SHEPHERDING?

The Bible is full of passages about shepherds and sheep. Many times the Old Testament will depict God Himself as the Shepherd of His people, Israel.

Behold, the Lord God shall come with a strong hand... He will feed His flock like a shepherd; He will gather the lambs with this arm, and carry them in His bosom, and gently lead those who are with young (Isaiah 40:10-11).

Jesus in the New Testament uses two descriptive illustrations where He declares Himself as the door of the sheep and the "good shepherd" (see John 10:7-16). But in addition to the Bible revealing that the God of Israel and Jesus Christ are shepherds, God in the Old Testament and Jesus in the New Testament have also appointed individuals to be leaders and shepherds to God's flock. Sheep who are called by God become used in the role of shepherd.

Traditionally, when a Christian thinks about someone becoming a shepherd, he or she probably thinks, "Oh, so they're going to become a pastor." Yes, in the New Testament this Greek word *poimen* can be translated as either pastor or shepherd depending on the context.

In the passage of Ephesians 4:11-12, this word is translated by the New King James version as "pastor."

And He Himself gave some to be apostles, some prophets, some evangelists, and some pastors and teachers, for the equipping of the saints for the work of the ministry, for the edifying of the body of Christ.

But did you notice that the apostles, prophets, evangelists, and teachers are also used for equipping believers and strengthening the Body of Christ? The functions of shepherding include all of the callings of God that have to do with ministering to the needs of the sheep. In other words, you do not necessarily have to be a "pastor" to be doing some function of shepherding in the Body of Christ or to those who are lost. So what does a biblical shepherd do exactly?

The very foundation of what shepherding looks like can be found with David's revelation of the Lord as his shepherd in Psalm 23:1. In this passage, it becomes clear to me that shepherding is about helping others with their physical needs as well as their spiritual needs. I believe with all my heart that God takes a holistic approach to helping people. Look at the first three verses of Psalm 23:

> *The Lord is my shepherd. I shall not be in want. He makes me lie down in green pastures, He leads me beside quiet waters, He restores my soul. He guides me in paths of righteousness for his name's sake* (Psalm 23:1-3).

Because the Lord is a good shepherd, David knows that he's not going to be in want. He's not going to be in distress because his physical needs aren't being met.

Verses 2 and 3 speak to me about the fact that the Lord is concerned about David feeling physically rested, emotionally stable, and spiritually restored. Not only that, but God is going to lead David down the right paths of decision making. He's going to guide him in the ways of right living and right thinking. He wants David to make good choices that will honor His name and keep His commandments. These are the characteristics of what a good shepherd does. Any person functioning as a shepherd will love people in this way and care for sheep by helping individuals at their point of need, whether it's physical, emotional, or spiritual.

In the old-school, non-digital world of photography, there has always been technology that can take negative film and develop its positive image. In Zechariah 11, there is a passage that's packed with spiritual insight, but its description of what a shepherd is supposed to do is given to us in the negative. It doesn't take much thinking or ingenuity to figure out what the positive is supposed to look like, whether we're looking at negative film or words of criticism. When Jesus chastised the church in Ephesus, He told them that He had this against them: that they had left their first love (see Rev. 2:4). He goes on to tell them to repent, and I believe that Jesus knew that His people had enough intelligence to get the positive flip side of what they needed to do without saying it again in the positive. They needed to return to their first love. So let's look at Zechariah 11:16 and then develop its negatives into its positive flip side.

For I [the Lord] *am going to raise up a shepherd over the land who will not care for the lost, or seek the young, or heal the injured, or feed the Healthy, but will eat the meat of the choice sheep, tearing off their hoofs* (Zechariah 11:16 NIV).

In its historical context, the Lord God of Israel is saying earlier in chapter 11 that although He is their shepherd, His flock (Judah and Israel) detests Him, and He will no longer be their shepherd. So verse 16, in the negative, is a word of judgment from the prophet Zechariah on the chronic faithlessness of His people. God is pronouncing that He will raise up a shepherd who will not care for the flock of God in five areas of shepherding. This is a worthless shepherd who is not going to care about lost sheep, young lambs, sheep that are hurting, feeding the flock, or making sure that they are protected from exploitation. This shepherd is the antithesis—the very opposite—of what a good shepherd should be. I'm sure you can see some relevant applications for spiritual leaders here, especially if you flip the negative image and develop its positive image.

On the positive side, we can say that shepherds will go after lost sheep, seek out the young ones, heal the hurting, feed the flock, and protect them from physical and spiritual harm. Let's develop each of these five areas of shepherding.

> *On the positive side, we can say*
> *that shepherds will go after lost*
> *sheep, seek out the young ones, heal*
> *the hurting, feed the flock, and*
> *protect them from physical and*
> *spiritual harm.*

GOING AFTER LOST SHEEP

All we like sheep have gone astray; We have turned everyone to his own ways and the Lord has laid on Him, the iniquity of us all (Isaiah 53:6).

From Genesis to Revelation, the pages of the Bible continually reveal that it is deep in the heart of God to redeem a people for Himself; to seek and save those who are lost. This is why He sent His only Son, Jesus, to fulfill the prophecies of Isaiah 53 and to die on a Roman cross for our sins. Jesus was sent from God to redeem us—to buy us back with His own blood.

Going after lost sheep is a super-objective of God. A super-objective is a main purpose of a person's mission or existence. Listen to the words of Jesus in Luke:

What man of you, having a hundred sheep, if he loses one of them, does not leave the ninety-nine in the wilder-

ness, and go after the one which is lost until he finds it?
And when he has found it, he lays it on his shoulders,
rejoicing. And when he comes home, he calls together his
friends and neighbors, saying to them: "Rejoice with me
for I have found my sheep which was lost!" I say to you
likewise there will be more joy in heaven over one sinner
who repents than over ninety-nine just persons who need
no repentance" (Luke 15:4-7).

Followers of Christ everywhere, with and without
formal Bible education, are being called on to do this in-
dispensable part of shepherding. If a person is usable, the
Holy Spirit will use that person to bring a lost sheep into
the Lord's fold. This is evangelism 101—to lead someone
to Christ.

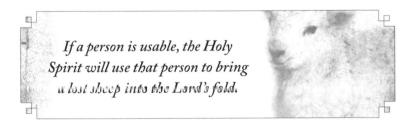

If a person is usable, the Holy
Spirit will use that person to bring
a lost sheep into the Lord's fold.

When I was around 18, I was raking leaves for old Mrs.
Brady. She was 93 and very set in her ways. I had a growing
feeling that she was spiritually lost. With every stroke of the
rake, I was praying for her. I said, "Lord, she's going to die
soon, and I don't know how to do this personal evangelism
stuff with an elderly woman. If I start talking to her about

Jesus, she is going to bite my head off. So Lord, if you want me to speak to her, then please make a way for me."

As soon as I finished praying, the screen door opened and Mrs. Brady invited me inside for ginger ale. As we sat at the kitchen table, she said to me, "You know, Rick, I'm going to die soon." So I said, "Well, we're all going to die, Mrs. Brady." I knew that she had gone to church all of her life, so I had to be careful how I worded what I was about to say next. I said, "You know there are some Christians who know where they are going when they die, and there are some that aren't really sure where they're going when they die." Well, she immediately put herself in the category of Christians who weren't sure where they were going when they die. I said, "Mrs. Brady, you can know for sure that you will go to Heaven. The Bible says:

> *God so loved the world that He gave His only son, Jesus, that whoever believes in Him will not die but will have eternal life* (John 3:16).

"If you want, let's hold hands and pray for Jesus to forgive all your sins and come into your heart as your Lord and Savior." She said, "I'd like that." So we held hands, and as we prayed for Jesus to come into her heart, the presence of the Holy Spirit seemed to be all around us. She thanked me for praying with her, and as I went out the door, I thanked God for helping me and using me for His purposes.

Mrs. Brady died one week later.

SHEEP FACT:

Young lambs are known for being incredibly stupid and can be found eating dirt or getting their heads stuck in fences.

SEEKING OUT THE YOUNG

After reading several books and articles on sheep, I found that the one thing that all shepherds seem to agree on is that young lambs are incredibly stupid. Sometimes they have to be shown how to get out of the barn in order to find their feeder. They may eat dirt or follow others without thinking about where they are headed. If a little lamb falls in a ditch or gets its head stuck in the fence, then somebody has to seek him out and help him.

Whether we are talking about children and youth, or older believers who are young spiritually, I believe that both groups of individuals need special care and attention from shepherding Christians. The immature need to be sought out and cared for at their point of need. If children in the city are poor and hungry, then let's get out the peanut butter and jelly sandwiches or have a pizza party. Invite them to church or to special events, meet some physical needs, give them a safe environment, make it fun, and always help them to follow Jesus. Children's church, Sunday school, and youth groups all come under the Zechariah 11:16 umbrella of what shepherding is supposed to be.

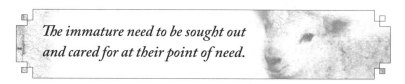

The immature need to be sought out and cared for at their point of need.

Extra efforts also have to be made for those who are spiritual infants or maybe developing toddlers. When people first give their lives to Jesus Christ, or when they never quite grow into spiritual maturity, the Bible says that they are babes in Christ. Paul recognized the spiritual immaturity of the believers at Corinth. *And I, brethren, could not speak to you as spiritual people but as to carnal, as to babes in Christ* (1 Cor. 3:1).

The believers at Corinth were acting immature because they were causing divisions and fighting. Personally, I've seen church business meetings so intense that I thought that fist fights were about to break out. Those who are more spiritually mature need to be leading by example and encouraging others to grow up in Christ. The more "shepherd-like" role models there are in a community of believers the better. Looking out for young Christians can often be too big of a task to be put solely on the shoulders of the local pastor. I've seen a number of non-staff church members who, on a regular basis, would take it upon themselves to check up on Christians who were becoming increasingly absent from Sunday services. I've even seen everyday church members volunteer to start foundational Bible classes after the church had a surge of new believers. These Christians are the mature sheep of the fold that are starting to morph into shepherds. They are losing the "what about me" type of mentality and beginning to seek out and help the younger sheep.

HEALING THE SICK AND INJURED

In the natural, I've read that about half of all lamb deaths occur because of two basic causes: overexposure to a cold environment and starvation. They become victims to hypothermia and die because there's no sustainable heat. In the spiritual, the sheep who have decided to follow Jesus need a place to come in from the cold world and get a good meal. Warmth and heat come from an environment where God's presence can kindle a flame in the believer. This can be any place or event where the Holy Spirit is welcomed and the burning embers of the gathering are fanned into a fire of revival and personal renewal. This place could be a church on Sunday morning, a night of worship and praise, a small group gathering, or a Christian special event. Shepherds who care about sheep will pray for God's presence to come to a meeting or event, and then they will invite the strays, the sick, and the frozen in heart.

The other half of the equation is to keep sheep healthy and warm by feeding them a healthy diet of good food on a regular basis. God's word is spiritual food for us. Going without regular feedings can result in spiritual hypothermia and indifference toward the things of God. Sheep and especially lambs need to be brought to the feeding trough. They need personal Bible study, group Bible study, Sunday sermons, and conference speakers. Jesus quoted Deuteronomy 8:3 when he was tempted by satan in the wilderness.

But he answered and said, "It is written: Man shall not live by bread alone, but by every word that proceeds from the mouth of God" (Matthew 4:4).

If sheep are going to eat spiritual food, then they are going to be consumers of God's written word. Jesus specifically tasked Peter with taking on the ministry of feeding sheep and caring for Christ's flock. In John 21:15-17, Jesus reinstates Peter after the resurrection by asking Peter if he loved Him and then commissions Peter by telling him to feed His lambs, take care of His sheep, and then, feed His sheep. Jesus knew that the feeding of His sheep is fundamental to their spiritual health and core temperature.

Just as sheep can get injured physically and become in need of a shepherd's hand, so too, Christians can become injured spiritually and will need the help of a shepherd-like friend. Oftentimes, a Christian will get into trouble spiritually when he or she has been hurt or offended by someone. The wounds could come from family, a spouse, a friend, or even those in the church. Wherever it comes from, the temptation is to become bitter and possibly even angry toward God. This starts a complete downward spiral in spiritual health. Furthermore, satan is opportunistic and will try to leverage the wound into an ongoing open sore that doesn't get a chance to heal. The enemy will use the Christian's hurt to turn him or her away from personal time with God, the warmth of Christian fellowship, and the regular feedings that come from personal Bible study and biblical teaching. Once isolation occurs in the life of the wounded Christian, spiritual coldness and acute hypothermia set in. Shepherds need to recognize the early warning signs of a wounded believer and pray for both their emotional and spiritual healing.

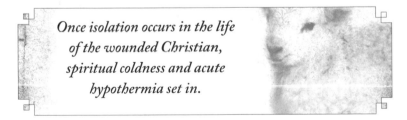

Once isolation occurs in the life of the wounded Christian, spiritual coldness and acute hypothermia set in.

FEEDING THE HEALTHY

Shepherds of real sheep understand that feeding sheep is the most critically important task that a shepherd can do. Chuck Wooster, in his book *Living with Sheep* said this about feeding his sheep:

Get it right, and your animals will be happy and healthy. Get it wrong, and your sheep will turn up with an amazing assortment of seemingly unrelated maladies; from bloating in summer, to freezing in the winter, to problems with lambing, hooves and lameness.[1]

Spiritually speaking, feeding the healthy is all about teaching and preaching from God's Word to committed believers. Get it right and you will be promoting sound doctrine and spiritual strength. Get it wrong, and you could be the source for a wide range of unhealthy beliefs, spiritual hypothermia, and damaging error. It's not in the scope of this book to write about good exegesis of Scripture and sound interpretation, but let's just say that Christians who are called to be shepherds need to be careful about what they are feeding the flock and maybe what they are not feeding the flock. Paul wrote to Timothy and said:

> *Be diligent to present yourself approved to God, a worker who does not need to be ashamed, rightly dividing the word of truth* (2 Timothy 2:15).

Those who are doing the feeding of the flock will obviously include teachers and pastors, but would also include not only Bible study facilitators and small group leaders but virtually anyone who is influencing others to grow strong in Christ through reading, writing, speaking, or explaining the Bible.

PROTECTION FROM ABUSE

Books that are about caring for real sheep all seem to have at least one chapter on dealing with predators and how to protect sheep from abuse. In the natural, predators kill sheep and carry away lambs. There are a few suggestions that seem to make sense for both natural and spiritual caretakers. Shepherds need to confront and resist the oncoming predators, much like David of the Bible confronted his enemies. Somebody needs to protect the sheep from abuse and take a stand. The apostle Paul did this when he wrote to the Galatians and confronted those who were promoting legalism. Good shepherds never compromise the Gospel and can be tenaciously confrontational when believers are threatened by cult-like ideas or off-the-wall teachings that will either fleece the flock, lead sheep astray, or bring believers into some kind of bondage.

Good shepherds never compromise the Gospel and can be tenaciously confrontational when believers are threatened by cult-like ideas or off-the-wall teachings that will either fleece the flock, lead sheep astray, or bring believers into some kind of bondage.

Other sheep-care suggestions for discouraging predators like wolves would include: using lots of lighting around the sheep pen perimeter, making sure that boundaries are marked, and making sure that the fencing is predator-tight. In the spiritual, using and reinforcing God's written Word acts like a high beam whose light can expose gross error, as well as provide fencing that guides sheep into righteous living and right thinking. Wandering outside God's fencing parameters of Scripture can not only lead sheep away from the Lord, but it can also make the believer more vulnerable to deception or a predator's sneak attack. *Your enemy the devil prowls around like a roaring lion looking for someone to devour* (1 Peter 5:8 NIV).

God's great desire is to have more shepherds and take more of His sheep on the path of becoming shepherds. In Psalm 23 we saw that the Lord's approach to taking care of David was to take care of the whole person. David's spiritual and physical needs were wonderfully met because that's the way the Lord does shepherding. Would it make any sense for the Body of Christ to take care of people spiritually but neglect the other pressing needs, like hunger or sickness?

There are a variety of ways for shepherds to take care of the needs of sheep. As we become conscious of others' needs, we may be called to seek out those who are lost, help those who are young, heal the injured, feed the healthy, or protect those who may be exposed to predators and abuse. There's no greater calling from God than to be called to do the work of a shepherd. I want to encourage you to seek God in prayer and ask Him if He would call you to a life of shepherding, in Jesus' name.

Points to Ponder

1. According to Chapter 1, who should be doing the work of shepherding God's flock and why?

_____

_____

_____

2. What is the biblical prerequisite for God's calling to shepherd and get assignments from the Holy Spirit?

_____

_____

_____

3. Is going from a consuming sheep to useful shepherd something that is only for those who want to be pastors?

_____

_____

_____

4. What kind of insight does Psalm 23 give us about the Lord as our Shepherd?

_____

_____

_____

5. What five categories of shepherd tasks does Zechariah 11:16 give us when we flip its negative description of bad shepherding into its positive equivalent?

_____

_____

_____

6. One of God's super-objectives is to seek and save lost sheep. In the story of Mrs. Brady, why was she lost, and how did she become found?

_____

_____

_____

ENDNOTE

1. Chuck Wooster, *Living with Sheep* (Guilford, Connecticut: The Lyons Press, 2005), 43.

Chapter 2

MOVE THAT CHAIR

*F*orty minutes from the George Washington Bridge and New York City is the small suburban town of Ramsey, New Jersey, where I spent my childhood. Beautiful trees lined its streets and would turn colors every fall, and with every new school year I would get a new set of clothes at Irv Learners. In the spring, my older brother Bill and I would play little league at Finch Park, and in the summer our family would take trips to either Tulip Lake or the Jersey Shore. It was a classic American upbringing, except for the occasional family flare-ups because of my Dad's affinity for closing business deals over a three-martini lunch. We didn't really talk much about God or pray at mealtimes, but Mom or Dad would drop me off for Sunday school at the

First Presbyterian Church of Ramsey, and this is where I learned about God and a number of Bible stories. Up until sixth grade, I understood the universe and was a very content kid.

I don't remember what exactly triggered it, but as an eleven-year-old I began to question everything, including the existence of God. It was a winter's day in December, and I remember walking past all the downtown Christmas decorations and the full-scale nativity scene in front of the Lutheran Church and thinking to myself, *What if God isn't real? What if there is no God?* That very thought threw me into a depression. Here it was Christmas time and I was having doubts about God's existence and feeling a kind of despair that I had never felt before. It felt like I was lost. After a few days of this, I decided to throw up a challenge. This one afternoon I stood alone in the family room, pointed my face to the ceiling, and said, "God, if you're real, then move this chair." I tried this "pray and then stare at the chair" technique several times, and after about ten minutes I gave up. This experiment was a complete bust, and I was even more despondent about the prospect that there might not be a God than I was before. What I didn't realize is that God will honor and respond to any person's feeble attempt to find Him, and that included my desperate prayer for the chair to move. What I really wanted was proof of His existence and more specifically, that He cared about me.

That night I remember going to bed, and in the darkness of my room I sensed a wonderful presence that surrounded me, and I not only knew that there was a God but also that He loved me and cared about me. How did I know? I just knew. He was in the room and He was awesome! Although God was not going to answer my test by moving the chair, He saw my heart and answered my prayer by paying me a visit in my bedroom. That night was one of my earliest encounters with the Holy Spirit, and since then I have experienced His love and His presence hundreds of times. Looking back on that night, I'm reminded of the passage, *"For he who comes to God must believe that He is, and that He is a rewarder of those who diligently seek Him"* (Heb. 11:6). God will always reward anyone who will actively pursue Him. And He especially blesses those who may seek Him while doubting, or who might even ask Him to move a chair.

Although God was not going to answer my test by moving the chair, He saw my heart and answered my prayer by paying me a visit in my bedroom.

GOD LOVES DOUBTERS

Typically people who have doubts about God will say that He may not exist, but at the same time will confess that if He does exist, then He's probably angry with them because they're having doubts in the first place. Nothing could be further from the truth. God loves doubters. For starters, most doubters are not so hard-core as to believe conclusively that there is no God. My father used to say that there are no atheists in foxholes. Foxholes are holes dug by soldiers who get in them in order to protect themselves from intense enemy fire. If you find yourself in one, then chances are you're pretty scared about coming out of the situation alive. Even the proclaimed atheist will usually hedge his bets and pray.

During seasons of catastrophe like Hurricane Katrina, the 2004 Indian Ocean tsunamis, or the devastating 2010 earthquake in Haiti, I'll listen to news releases on all the major networks like ABC, CNN, Fox News, or BBC, and suddenly everyone is talking about praying and God. Unfortunately, when things begin to settle down, people tend to put God on the back burner. But during those times of seeking out God, He is always faithful to respond to people, and He welcomes doubters. This is the first baby step in not only discovering God as a lost sheep, but the first step toward peace with God by responding to His invitation of eternal life through His Son Jesus. Listen to His invitation.

For God so loved the world that He gave His only begotten Son, that whoever believes in Him should not perish but have everlasting life (John 3:16).

This is probably the most famous verse in the Bible, but it's well worth repeating because it explains so much so succinctly; and it's a personal invitation on an epic scale, like when someone gives a marriage proposal on one knee. The fact that He loves you, that He sacrificed His Son for you, and that His hope is for you to believe and not doubt, is huge.

Thomas, even though he was one of the original 12 disciples, is the Bible's poster child for not believing in the resurrection and is remembered through the ages as "doubting Thomas." And yet Jesus loved Him, worked with him, and invited him to believe.

Jesus Didn't Reject Thomas for Doubting

Jesus' reaction to Thomas's doubts shows us that Jesus welcomes skeptics and doubters. Thomas didn't see Jesus on the day that He was resurrected, so naturally the other disciples had the advantage of seeing their Lord alive. Notice that Jesus not only did not reject Thomas but invited him to explore his apprehensions.

Now Thomas, called the twin, one of the twelve, was not with them when Jesus came. The other disciples therefore said to him, "We have seen the Lord." So he said to them,

"Unless I see in His hands the print of the nails, and put my hand into His side, I will not believe." And after eight days His disciples were again inside, and Thomas with them. Jesus came, the doors being shut and stood in the midst, and said, "Peace to you!" Then He said to Thomas, "Reach your finger here, and put it into My side. Do not be unbelieving, but believing." And Thomas answered and said to Him, "My Lord and my God!" Jesus said to him, "Thomas, because you have seen Me, you have believed. Blessed are those who have not seen and yet have believed" (John 20:24-29).

The story of doubting Thomas reminds me of a story about a high school science teacher who announced just before Easter break that the Easter story was nothing but a fabrication and a myth. He went on to say that Jesus was not raised from the dead and that there's no God in Heaven who would allow His Son to be nailed to a Roman cross. A student in the third row whose name was Michael raised his hand and said, "Teacher, I believe in God, and I believe in the resurrection." The teacher responded, "Michael, you can believe whatever you want to believe in, but there's no conclusive proof that God exists. The miracle of the resurrection is a scientific impossibility. No one who believes in miracles can also be a good student of science."

Opening the classroom refrigerator, the science teacher found a raw egg and decided to conduct an experiment.

He held up the egg and said, "Class, I'm going to drop this egg on the floor, and when I do, gravity will drop it to the ground and the egg will break apart." Turning to Michael, the teacher challenged him and said, "Here's what I want you to do, Michael. I want you to pray a prayer in front of the class and ask your God to keep this egg from breaking. When this egg in my hand hits the floor, it will not break. If your God can keep it from breaking, then you will have proved that there is a God and I'll have to admit that you were right and I was wrong."

Michael thought about the challenge for a minute, stood at his desk, and began to pray. "Dear Heavenly Father, I pray that when my teacher drops the egg, that it will break into a hundred pieces. And Lord, I also pray that when the egg breaks, my teacher will have a heart attack and die. Amen." After a collective "whoa" from the class, everyone waited and watched for the egg to drop. The teacher just stood there for a minute. Then he looked at Michael and then the floor. Without saying a word, the teacher put the egg back in the refrigerator. He dismissed the class and slowly sat down at his desk. The teacher wasn't ready to put his life on the line to prove that God didn't exist. In other words, deep down he was considering the possibility that God did exist, and if there was the slightest chance that He did, then the science teacher needed to hedge his bets, put the egg back, and not take a chance that Michael's prayer would be answered.

It's all right to have questions or reservations about God and the supernatural. Sometimes people need to doubt and have questions before they come to the point of believing. These are often the early steps that lead to an encounter with the Living God. If you are at this stage in your journey, then I would like to invite you to ask God if He would reveal Himself to you. Seek Him out, and don't be surprised when He answers you. God loves you very much and wants you to believe and have a relationship with Him through Jesus, His Son. Remember that the Bible teaches this one great truth throughout its pages: that it's in the heart of the Father to bring home lost sheep.

It's all right to have questions or reservations about God and the supernatural. Sometimes people need to doubt and have questions before they come to the point of believing.

Points to Ponder

1. Hebrews 11:6 tells us that God will reward those who diligently seek Him. What kind of reward does God give the seeker?

_____

_____

_____

2. Do you believe that there are no atheists in foxholes? Why or why not?

_____

_____

_____

3. If you were Thomas in the Bible, how would you have responded to feeling Jesus' nail-scarred hands and pierced side? How did Thomas respond?

_____

_____

_____

4. Have you ever talked to someone who had doubts about the existence of God? What did you say to him or her? If you have never talked to someone with doubts about God, what might you say to him or her?

_____

_____

_____

Chapter 3

LOST SHEEP FOUND

As a sixteen-year-old, I was soaking in the culture and music of the early seventies. I loved to follow what we used to call "FM" rock: music by Jimi Hendrix, Crosby, Stills, Nash, and Young, and any music with lyrics that reinforced the values and behavior of the popular hippie culture. Actually, a lot of us were part-time, wannabe hippies. I played bass in a high school rock band, but I also played on the high school football team. I would get high on Saturday, but I lived at home and I would hide my bag of pot in a raccoon hat above the shoe boxes in my bedroom closet. My hair was a little long but not long enough to make my dad go ballistic. And even though I was totally lost spiritually, I was one of those non-followers of Jesus Christ who was pretty happy with my life. There were no major crises in my life, but I was still far away from God.

Two blocks down from Ramsey High School in Ramsey, New Jersey, was a popular high school hangout called Rita's Sweet Shoppe. I went to Rita's after school, and as I sat on a counter stool slurping my coffee and enjoying the juke box, in walked a senior who most of us knew as a really good bass player. His name was Barry Gretz, and he was used by God that day to start me on a spiritual journey that culminated in a decision to give my life to Jesus Christ. I said, "How are you doin', Barry?" He was so effusive and began to tell me that Jesus had changed his life. He said that he was playing in a new rock band called Maranatha, and he invited me to see him play that Friday night at a Church of the Nazarene in New Milford, New Jersey. I decided to go check his band out.

That Friday night, April 9, 1971, I walked toward the Church of the Nazarene where Barry was playing, and I found myself amazed by the experience of it all. This was a church that could sit about 200, and yet there were a lot more people there than that! The inside sanctuary was full, the basement was packed, and there were high school and college age people all over the outside lawn. The presence of the Holy Spirit was so strong, and everyone I met seemed to be as excited about living for Jesus as Barry was.

Out on the lawn, I was invited to make the same decision they had made. They asked me if I wanted to say yes
to Jesus Christ and to thank Him for dying on a cross for
my sins. I had two things going on inside of me at the same
time. On the one hand, there was a powerful feeling and
an invisible presence that felt like liquid love. It was an incredibly wonderful feeling that was encouraging me to take
the plunge. The Holy Spirit was wooing me. On the other
hand, I was somehow acutely aware of the fact that if I gave
my life to Jesus I was going to be giving up a lifestyle of
weekend binging and chasing after parties. I might end up
losing some friends in this deal. And even though I was
not at the end of my rope, my desire for getting right with
God became greater and more important than anything I
could ever give up. On this warm April night in 1971, I sat
in a circle holding hands with other new Christians, and I
bowed my head and gave my heart to Jesus.

BORN-AGAIN GROWING PAINS

I was on a spiritual high that lasted into the next few
weeks. I found myself having a new set of priorities, new
values, new appetites, and a new relationship with Jesus
Christ. It seemed like everything was brand-new. I was born
again. In God's eyes, I was the lost sheep that became found.
By one sincere prayer of faith, I had walked through the
door and into the light of God's goodness and favor. I was
completely saved.

Then Jesus said to them again, "Most assuredly, I say to you, I am the door of the sheep. All who ever came before Me are thieves and robbers, but the sheep did not hear them. I am the door. If anyone enters by Me, he will be saved, and will go in and out and find pasture…I have come that they might have life and that they may have it more abundantly" (John 10:7-10).

Remember when I was on the church lawn and wondering if I would lose some friends if I gave my life to Christ? I had a best friend named Frank who refused to come with me to Maranatha or any other Christian place. We used to have in common a party-till-you-puke outlook on life, but now we had very little in common. He became hostile toward me and in a sardonic and bitter tone would say to me, "How you doin', God?" There is a price to pay for following Christ, but it is so small in comparison to the price that He paid to ransom me from sin and death. I hope and pray that someday Frank will have a change of heart and give his life to Jesus.

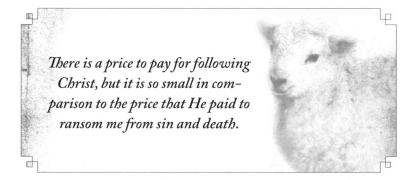

There is a price to pay for following Christ, but it is so small in comparison to the price that He paid to ransom me from sin and death.

Not only did this decision to give my life to Jesus have an impact on my social life, but it also created new problems with my family. My enthusiasm for the Bible and for going to meetings caught my Dad's attention. I remember talking to him while he was shaving one morning. With steam rising up from the sink, he said to me, "Why do you have to go to so many religious meetings? I mean a little religion is OK, but you're going way overboard on this." We had daily discussions about Jesus and God, and I shared with him the difference between having "head knowledge" about God and really knowing Him. Six months later, my Dad was driving to a sales call, he stopped at a railroad crossing where the freight cars were creeping along at a turtle's pace, bowed his head at the steering wheel, and asked Jesus to come into his life. That was the end of his Monday through Friday habit of coming home inebriated, and it began a new chapter of closeness between him and my Mom.

There are two kinds of sheep out there: lost sheep and found sheep. The night that I gave my life to Jesus was the rescue point for me. I had gone from darkness to light and from death to life. I went from being a lost sheep to being found of God, and I became born again. Jesus told his friend Nicodemus that he must be born again. *"Jesus answered and said to him, "Most assuredly, I say to you, unless one is born again, he cannot see the kingdom of God"* (John 3:3). This is the entry point that everyone needs to begin life as a sheep in Christ's fold. If this has never been your experience, please don't put it off. I urge you to thank God for sending His only Son, Jesus Christ, to die on a cross for your sins. Ask Him to forgive all that you've ever done wrong and to help you turn from any behavior that doesn't please Him. Ask Jesus to come into your life to be your Lord, your Savior, and your very best friend. If you have done this and you meant business with God, then congratulations; you are now a sheep in Christ's fold.

Points to Ponder

1. What's your story? How and when did you personally surrender your life to following after Jesus?

_____

_____

_____

2. As you began following Christ, how did your life change? What was new about your lifestyle?

_____

_____

_____

3. How did your family respond to your decision to follow Jesus? Were they supportive?

_____

_____

_____

4. Explain how a person can biblically transition from being a lost sheep to becoming a found sheep.

_____

_____

_____

Chapter 4

CAN YOU HEAR ME NOW?

Within a month or so I found myself playing bass in a Christian rock band called Salt of the Earth. The Jesus Movement revival of the seventies was crossing all denominational lines, and we were playing on Saturday night to a packed house in a Catholic facility in Park Ridge, New Jersey. Father Ken was on fire for the Lord and gave us complete freedom to preach about Jesus and ask for decisions to receive Christ. But the epicenter for the Jesus Movement in North Jersey was still Friday nights at the Church of the Nazarene in New Milford, New Jersey.

Reverend Paul Moore, who grew his hair long and wore a collar, jeans, and cowboy boots, would maintain the

Sunday services and perform the endless water baptisms in the church's above-ground swimming pool. And like Father Ken in Park Ridge, Paul Moore allowed Maranatha's lead guitarist Charlie Rizzo full freedom to speak about how Christ had delivered him from a life of drugs. Charlie would always follow his testimony with an invitation to receive Christ. It was in this environment that I began to sense a calling on my life. It was a feeling and a sense that God was going to call me into some kind of greater ministry, but there were no specifics.

Then came the spiritual warfare, and for a few months I regrettably returned to my old lifestyle of drinking and pot smoking. This is a very unhappy situation for a loud Christian to be in! I remember those who had heard my message and were now disgusted by my hypocrisy. I was a walking contradiction because I still believed, but I became entrapped by a sin lifestyle and it was very hard to stop. Later on I began to understand a verse in Ephesians that says, *"And do not give the devil a foothold"* (Eph. 4:27 NIV). By saying yes to the temptation, I had given the devil a foothold. The devil was like a door-to-door salesman who was just waiting for me to open the door a little, and then get his foot in the jam so he could open it some more. Because of my decisions to sin, I had allowed the enemy a foothold in my life. I had given him permission to mess with me and entangle me all over again.

It was so hard to stop, and I remember crying out to God alone in my parents' living room. I said, "Jesus, there's no one here to lay hands on me and help me, so right now would You lay hands on me?" I knew that there was no chapter and verse for a prayer like this, but I just desperately wanted freedom from this new grip that sin had over my life. I don't know exactly what happened in the spiritual realm, but I do know that after I prayed this desperate prayer, I felt His presence all over me. At that moment, I had returned from my backslidden state and found myself broken, humbled, and joyfully in love with the Lord again. I told Jesus that I wanted to serve Him again, and even though I would love to serve by playing bass in a Christian band, I would be willing to scrub toilets or be a missionary to a country that doesn't even have any toilets.

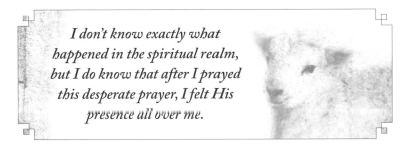

I don't know exactly what happened in the spiritual realm, but I do know that after I prayed this desperate prayer, I felt His presence all over me.

In less than a week, I was asked by singer Lillian Parker if I would like to be the replacement for the bass player of a Christian band called Burning Bush. For the next two years I served the Lord as their bass player performing in churches, coffee houses, and outdoor concerts. I was being used again for evangelism. The sense of calling to greater ministry that had left me when I fell away suddenly returned to me again, yet nothing specific.

"I'm sensing some kind of general calling, so Lord, what would you like me to do?" I asked. I didn't know exactly what direction I was supposed to go in, but undaunted, I entered Nyack College as a commuting freshman, and the following year I continued my education by attending and eventually graduating from Elim Bible Institute in Lima, New York. Still there was no specific calling to be a pastor, a teacher, a missionary, or maybe an evangelist.

With hindsight, I now know that the delay in my specific calling was due to the fact that I would only live committed to the Lord during the academic year and I would lose that commitment every summer. I wasn't reliable. I was not consistently faithful during times of temptation or when there was a vacation from living in a "fishbowl," Bible school environment. I was a seasonal Christian, and I was prone to take the path of least resistance.

Despite the roller coaster ride of my Christian life, God had helped me with some unexpected money to transfer my credits to Southern California College (now Vanguard University) and get a bachelor's degree in biblical studies. Most Christian colleges like Southern California College (SCC) have, to a greater or lesser degree, groups of people who represent the entire spectrum of Christian commitment: from those that are sold-out for Jesus to those that are fallen away and some who are just lost. Students can choose to be influenced by either those who are committed on campus to following Christ or by those who are not committed. I became influenced by the latter, and by the time of my graduation from SCC, I was entering into another backsliding episode in my life. The sense of calling from God seemed to be lost again. Losing that sense of calling is a bit like getting a call on your cell phone, and as the signal strength becomes weaker, the call is dropped. There's no communication because there's no signal.

> *Losing that sense of calling is a bit like getting a call on your cell phone, and as the signal strength becomes weaker, the call is dropped.*

The very first invitation that we get from the Lord is the call to salvation. Peter expressed it in First Peter 2:9-10 as being called out of darkness and into His marvelous light where we receive mercy.

> *But you are a chosen generation, a royal priesthood, a holy nation, His own special people, that you may proclaim the praises of Him, who called you out of darkness into His marvelous light; who once were not a people but are now the people of God, who had not obtained mercy but now have obtained mercy* (1 Peter 2:9-10).

When somebody hears the good news of Jesus Christ, he or she has a choice to heed the call and accept the invitation to follow Him or to say no to the call. Jesus said in John:

> My sheep hear my voice and I know them and they follow me and I give them eternal life and they shall never perish, neither shall anyone snatch them out of my hand (John 10:22:28).

All of Jesus' disciples were called to follow Him, yet it wasn't until after the resurrection that, except for Judas, they were all commissioned to begin their ministry of making disciples of all nations. Jesus hinted at the future calling of Peter in Luke 22:23, *"But I (Jesus) have prayed for you, that your faith should not fail; and when you have returned to Me, strengthen your brethren."*

Peter was going to have a falling away from following Christ, and later Jesus was going to introduce Peter to another calling: a shepherd's calling that was in addition to the initial calling to follow Jesus. After Jesus was resurrected and Peter was following the Lord again, Jesus gave Peter in John 21 a more specific calling of becoming a shepherd.

> So when they had eaten breakfast, Jesus said to Simon Peter, "Simon, son of Jonah, do you love Me more than these?" He said to Him, "Yes, Lord, you know that I love you." He said to him, "Feed my lambs." He said to him

*again a second time, "Simon, son of Jonah, do you love
Me?" He said to Him, "Yes Lord; You know that I love
you." He said to him, "Tend My sheep." He said to him
the third time, "Simon, son of Jonah, do you love Me?"
Peter was grieved because He said to him the third time.
"Do you love me?" And he said to Him, "Lord, you know
all things; You know that I love you." Jesus said to him
"Feed My sheep"* (John 21:15-17).

Peter was being called to be a shepherd. All of us are
called to accept and follow Christ as Lord and Savior first
and foremost, but the other calling to the work of a shepherd comes from the Lord also and is contingent upon our
faithfulness. Chapter 7 will illustrate this faithfulness factor
even further with a parable I've called "the Wal-Mart Principle." Salvation always needs to be followed with discipleship, and the discipleship end-game is to be called by the
Holy Spirit into useful service.

*All of us are called to accept and
follow Christ as Lord and Savior
first and foremost, but the other
calling to the work of a shepherd
comes from the Lord also and is
contingent upon our faithfulness.*

Points to Ponder

1. Author Rick Tunis experienced the revival known as the Jesus Movement. Have you ever seen or experienced a move of God?

_____

_____

_____

2. What happens to a follower of Jesus Christ when he or she gives in to a temptation?

_____

_____

_____

3. Have you ever felt in a general sense that God is calling you toward some kind of ministry in life?

_____

_____

_____

4. What are the two callings of God?

_____

_____

_____

5. How can Christians who are college students protect themselves from spiritual compromise?

_____

_____

_____

6. If salvation needs to be followed by discipleship, then discipleship needs to be followed by what?

_____

_____

_____

Part Two:

Falling Away from
Following

Chapter 5

YO-YO CHRISTIANITY

I have learned from personal experience that having one foot inside the kingdom sheep pen and another foot outside of the Lord's perimeter fencing is no way to go through life as a Christian. Once I began to compromise my commitment to Christ, I would find myself either spiritually up or spiritually down during any given week or day. Allowing myself to indulge in certain pet sins was the down cycle, but feeling guilty and remembering the goodness of the Lord would usually bring me back to asking Jesus for forgiveness and starting all over again, like the fall and rise of a yo-yo.

My senior year in college showed me that even at a Christian college there can be an unofficial group of backsliders and lightly committed believers who will give you that false sense of community within the greater college community. As I became familiar with these students, it became easier to be tempted in a variety of ways. I would learn about secular concerts and parties off campus, or I would occasionally be invited to get high with someone. There were other temptations to deal with as well: sex, gossip, and a return to worldly values. Much of my twenties became a crazy up-and-down spiritual roller coaster of falling into sin and coming back to the Lord.

On the "yo-yo down cycle," I would experience a lack of closeness and relationship with Jesus. Worldly thinking would replace godly thinking. It's like taking the fruits of the Spirit and putting them in reverse. Inner peace goes out the window, and thoughts of love and kindness are short-lived and easily exchanged for impatience and self-centeredness. Instead of having a passion for the Lord and the things of God, a pre-Christ mind-set would kick in. But during the yo-yo "up cycle," there would always be a restoration of my personal relationship with God. Why? Because of God's great promises and grace to forgive us. *If we confess our sins, He is faithful and just to forgive us our sins and to cleanse us from all unrighteousness* (1 John 1:9).

He is always faithful to His promises, and His love for us supersedes anything we may have done as an offense. I believe that there are tens of thousands of believers today who could be labeled as yo-yo Christians. They've had a close relationship with Jesus. At a special point in their lives, they bowed their heart, received forgiveness, and made a decision to follow Christ, but yielding to temptations and compromise has become their lifestyle ever since. For them, the Christian walk has been more of a running back and forth between living for God and living away from God than having that steady stride of faithfulness. Maybe you've met the yo-yo Christian. He or she is that unique breed of person who can speak "Christianese" and can argue with apologetic zeal about the merits of intelligent design but will query you as to whether or not you would be interested in smoking a bong after dinner and playing some video games later that night.

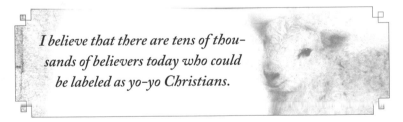

I believe that there are tens of thousands of believers today who could be labeled as yo-yo Christians.

When my kids were growing up, we would watch the movie *Hook* with Robin Williams as Peter Pan. I remember a scene where Peter Pan shows up and there is a showdown between Peter Pan and the lost boys' leader, Ruffio. Every time someone would give a reason for following Pan or Ruffio, all the lost boys would run to that leader. And so they would run back and forth until a line was finally drawn in the dirt and they ultimately chose Peter Pan to follow. That's the life of the yo-yo Christian. It's about always running back and forth between following Jesus and following the world. It's about having two alternating allegiances—one to the carnal nature and one to Christ. All too often the yo-yo Christian will make his or her moment-to-moment choices based on the path of least resistance. Any recommitment to Christ proves to be shallow or short-lived. The choice is always this: should I follow God and His Word, or should I follow what everybody around me is doing and thinking at the moment?

The people of Israel had a similar dilemma in front of them at Mount Carmel in First Kings 18.

And Elijah came to all the people, and said, "How long will you falter between two opinions? If the Lord is God, follow Him; but if Baal, follow him." But the people answered him not a word (1 Kings 18:21).

Elijah's showdown between himself and the 450 prophets of Baal began with the challenge that the people of God would stop running back and forth between two opinions about who to follow. Elijah then told the people to get two bulls. Then the prophets of Baal and Elijah were to each have a bull, cut it into parts, and lay it on the wood without any fire. Elijah told the Baal prophets to call on their gods and he would call on the name of the Lord, and the one who answers by fire is the real God. Elijah let the Baal prophets go all day long before taking his turn. The Baal followers yelled, they prophesied, they jumped up and down, they even cut themselves, but there was no answer. Then Elijah called God's people near and made his preparations. Just to make it an even more improbable miracle, Elijah dug a trench and had others fill four water pots with water and pour them on his altar. He had this repeated three times and then prayed a Spirit-inspired prayer that gives us rich insight into the heart of God as the loving father and shepherd of Israel. In verse 37 Elijah prays:

Hear me, O Lord, hear me, that this people may know that You are the Lord God, and that you have turned their hearts back to You again (1 Kings 18:37).

Elijah's prayer gives us the purpose of the showdown: to turn their hearts back to the Lord.

The next verse tells us that the fire of the Lord fell and consumed the sacrifice, the wood, and even the excess water. It was such an astonishing display of fire-power that the people fell on their faces and declared the winner—that the Lord, He is God!

It was such an astonishing display of fire-power that the people fell on their faces and declared the winner—that the Lord, He is God!

Sometimes it takes a showdown or a revelation of God's greatness to force a poorly committed believer out of complacency and back on the path of faithfulness. At least some, if not most, of Israel's motivation to return to God came from a new and acute understanding that the Lord is God Almighty and is not to be messed with. It's what the Bible calls having the fear of the Lord, and it's something that I had regained a greater knowledge of later in life. I'll explain my understanding of the fear of the Lord more completely in Chapter 6. Suffice it to say, this chapter represents the yo-yo period of my life with God where I did not have a consistent walk with the Lord. I had picked up an MFA from Colombia University, but I could not pick up the signal from God that I remembered having as a teenager.

> *At least some, if not most, of Israel's motivation to return to God came from a new and acute understanding that the Lord is God Almighty and is not to be messed with.*

Points to Ponder

1. Describe what is happening when someone begins to live like a yo-yo Christian.

_____

_____

_____

2. What Bible promise assures us that if we confess our sins, then God will forgive our sins and completely cleanse us? Can you think of any other passages in the Bible that speak about God's willingness to forgive us?

_____

_____

3. Why were the people of Israel faltering between two opinions in First Kings 18:21?

_____

_____

_____

4. Were the people of Israel being influenced to compromise, and if so, by whom?

_____

_____

_____

5. What was the purpose of Elijah's showdown with the prophets of Baal? What did God want to accomplish through Elijah?

_____

_____

_____

6. Can a yo-yo Christian be useful to God?

_____

_____

_____

Chapter 6

DRIFTING AWAY

The yo-yo Christian lifestyle of my twenties set me up for a complete drifting away in my thirties. Being a yo-yo Christian will do two things: it will make you only marginally useful to God during the up-cycle, and if not corrected, it will eventually escort you further and further away from the things of God until your past life with God becomes a distant memory. It's like leaving your home and living in a foreign country for several years. After a few years, your memories of home become a little hazy. In my late thirties, I remembered thinking thoughts that reflected how far away I had drifted from God. *Gee, I remember when I used to pray, when I used to read the Bible, and when I used to feel the presence of the Holy Spirit. I remember a long time ago that I was once used by God to lead others to Christ and I used to feel a sense of calling on my life. Yeah, I remember when I was close to Jesus.*

Being a yo-yo Christian will do two things: it will make you only marginally useful to God during the up-cycle, and if not corrected, it will eventually escort you further and further away from the things of God until your past life with God becomes a distant memory.

During an up-cycle in my twenties, I met my future wife, Nancy, and through our dating, she gave her heart to Jesus. After a few years, my devotion time with Nancy and with myself went away. I've learned from personal experience that cutting out prayer time and Bible reading from the routine of daily living is a recipe for spiritual disaster.

In my thirties, day-to-day "living away from God" developed into a way of life. I finished a six-year hitch in the Navy and left the military as a family of four. Nancy and I gained two terrific daughters while overseas. But it was in the Navy that I became a completely backslidden sheep. Returning to New Jersey, I brought back with me two habits from the Navy: drinking scotch on a daily basis and feeding my appetite for soft porn.

As I began to make a living as a sales representative for an industrial supplier, my spiritual condition went from bad to worse. My thought-life was becoming reprehensible. Even though I had a fantastic wife and two beautiful girls, lusting with my eyes became a constant indulgence. Worship was replaced by bombarding my mind with the latest music, and listening to shock-jock Howard Stern on the radio. I'm not a legalist with secular music, but some songs have a dark side, and in excess it can become a replacement for communing with the Lord. I was either thinking about sexual things or sales or sports or the latest "get rich quick" scheme. I actually bought Carlton Sheet's *How to Buy Real Estate with No Money Down*, but I never really got to the point of purchasing property that way.

My thoughts were not about how to please God or how to love others; my brain activity was all about me. *What can I do that's fun? What can I do after working hours that will entertain me or give me a rush? What about me?* It was a lifestyle of feeding my appetites for my own personal pleasure and gain. Except for an occasional flashback and twinge of guilt thinking about my earlier days of following Christ, the things of God were not on my radar screen. My life was filled with activities like coaching girls' softball, family road trips, and making a living; but spiritually I was completely adrift.

Therefore, we must give the more earnest heed to the things we have heard, lest we drift away (Hebrews 2:1).

I am making a distinction between life as a yo-yo Christian and life as someone who is drifting away from God. Drifting is backsliding at a whole new level. At least the yo-yo Christian has a sense of returning to the Lord when he or she fails or messes up his or her life. It's a matter of degree. The backslider who stops returning to the Lord has lost all mooring. Mooring is a nautical term, and it can be defined as the roping that holds a boat or ship to the dock. Any ship that loses its mooring is no longer attached to the dock and it will aimlessly drift out to sea. This is an even worse situation spiritually than running back and forth between a relationship with Jesus and following the world.

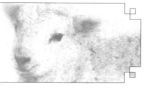

The backslider who stops returning to the Lord has lost all mooring.

Drifting from God is in my opinion best illustrated by the experience of the prodigal or lost son in Luke 15. In the parable of the lost son, Jesus says that the younger of the two sons asked for his inheritance prematurely. He packed his bags, left his father's house, and went to a far-away country for the purpose of spending his possessions on extravagant and wild living. In other words, he chose to live far away from his father's house, his love, and his care in order to spend what was given to him in a wasteful way. He drifted far from home and left all the benefits he had enjoyed when he was living in his father's house. And the most tragic thing of all was that he had severed his relationship with his father.

What do yo-yo Christianity and spiritual drifting analogies have to do with the shepherding metaphor? Christians as sheep are supposed to follow Christ their shepherd and grow up to be usable shepherds themselves. Paul longed for the believers at Galatia to reach this level of maturity:

My little children, for whom I labor in birth again until Christ is formed in you, I would like to be present with you now and to change my tone; for I have doubts about you (Galatians 4:19-20).

When Christ is formed in a believer, it's at this point that a Christian has the potential to become more useful to God and a candidate for divine promotion to greater ministry. Once the yo-yo cycle has been broken and the potential for drifting has been completely eliminated, then the call will come again and the believer will, in time, morph from being a sheep into being a shepherd for others.

Points to Ponder

1. What does the Bible say about drifting in Hebrews 2:1?

   _____

   _____

   _____

2. What does the author consider the forerunner to "drifting"? Why is it the forerunner to drifting?

   _____

   _____

   _____

3. When people drift from God, can they find inferior substitutes for their devotion time, worship, and fellowship? Give two or more examples.

   _____

   _____

   _____

4. According to Paul, were the Galatians mature Christians or immature? What needed to be formed in them? How can this be formed in us?

_____

_____

_____

_____

Chapter 7

JESUS IS MY SHEPHERD

*G*et the picture. I've been drifting away from God for about ten years. I had no church that I would go to, no devotional life, nothing. I was smoking two cigarette packs a day of Marlboro Red and going through a bottle of Dewar's scotch a week. My biggest sales account was about to close, and even though I saw it coming, I was too far away from God to feel at ease with asking Him for help.

Without so much as one thought of returning to Christ, I found myself standing in the kitchen and suddenly noticing the presence of the Lord. I remembered what His presence felt like from the time I sensed Him in my bedroom as a pre-teen, from the time I gave my life to Him as a teenager, when I served Him as a musician during the Jesus Movement, when

I soaked in His presence during times of worship, and when I sporadically followed Christ in my twenties. I felt awkward, ashamed, and blessed all at the same time.

I was given an impression that the Lord wanted me to give something to Elim Bible Institute. What kind of crazy impression is this? I would think that His reappearance into my life would include a laundry list of all the things that needed fixing. But the Holy Spirit was soft and gentle, and He wanted me to just take this one baby step of obedience. Still feeling His presence, I called for my wife, Nancy, who was in the living room. She came in, and I said, "Nance, I feel like God's telling me to give something to Elim Bible Institute. I know money is tight, but how about if we send a check for twenty-five dollars to them?" She agreed, and that little baby step of obedience set in motion an incredible series of events that put me back on the road to restoration and personal revival.

THE FEAR OF THE LORD

A day or so later, I found myself getting a very strong impression that I was spiritually in big trouble. I was a dry branch with no fruit; I was a yo-yo Christian in my twenties and had wasted away my thirties. I was guilty of disobeying His Word, and I had made a million choices that were wrong and damaging to both me and others. I was starting to understand the fear of the Lord, because I was becoming aware of how far away I was from His goodness. Like the prodigal son, I was starting to come to my senses. It was like I was in a far-away country, and I needed to somehow return to the Lord, if He would actually take me back. I even rehearsed what I would say to the Lord when the time was right. In Jesus' parable, the lost son did this, too.

> *I was starting to understand the fear of the Lord, because I was becoming aware of how far away I was from His goodness.*

Over the next couple of weeks, the Holy Spirit began to surgically remove certain sins that had been so deeply embedded into my thinking and lifestyle. There were two pet sins that I especially remember as detrimental to my spiritual walk with Christ: pornographic magazines and the recreational use of pot. During my years as a yo-yo Christian, I would default to one or both of these sins whenever there was an upheaval in my life or a period of spiritual dryness and temptation. For the first time, I recognized that I had been making destructive choices and that if I didn't turn my life around soon, then there was going to be a price tag for chronically choosing the wrong things. In addition to that, God's great plan for my life was put on a long hold. I'm so thankful and grateful that He knows how to pull us out of our own messes and that no mess is too big.

I was awakened at four o'clock in the morning by the strongest satanic presence I had ever felt in my life. It was like a blanket of fear; terror was draped over me. Jumping out of bed, I ran downstairs and groped for the Bible that we kept on the end table in the living room. I quickly turned on the lamp, and as I flipped through its pages, I tried to remember what I used to do back in the days when I had been following the Lord closely. I decided to speak to this demonic presence and said, "In the name of Jesus, I command you to leave." It didn't leave. I tried this two or three more times, but it just wasn't working.

I thought, *What am I going to do now?* I prayed and asked the Lord to help me and take this horrible presence off me. Just then it occurred to me that I should get rid of the dozen or so *Playboy* magazines that I had in the basement. I grabbed a Hefty bag from the kitchen, ran down the basement steps, and quickly threw the magazines into the dark green plastic opening. I pulled on the drawstring, tied it up, ran the bag back up the basement stairs, and threw it outside with the rest of the trash. Immediately the satanic presence left, and I was amazed at how fast it had disappeared. I now was beginning to associate obedience with spiritual protection and the porn magazines with that demonic presence. I vowed to myself that I would never, ever again even think about looking at this kind of stuff or even glancing at anything like it. My days as a consumer of porn were over.

Just a few days later, a woman in the purchasing department where I worked decided to treat me to a small bag of pot. Now I wasn't a regular smoker of marijuana, but without fail, if it was offered to me, I would take it and never think twice about using it. I thanked her and took it home to smoke that night. With the kids in bed, I sat on the couch in the living room and began to roll it with cigarette paper. I could hear one of the girls coming down the steps, so I hid the stash behind my back. Our oldest daughter, Colleen, was eight at the time, and as she came halfway down the stairs she looked afraid. I said, "What's wrong, honey?" and Colleen said to me words that I'll never forget. "Daddy, I can't sleep, and I'm scared. I keep thinkin' of the devil."

Having experienced my own recent encounter with demonic fear, how could I possibly be so calloused as to ignore my own daughter's plea for help? Could it be that my choices to sin were now providing a green light for demonic attacks on my family? I said to Colleen, "Honey, I'll be right up to pray with you." I went into the bathroom, flushed the pot down the toilet, and went upstairs to pray with my eight-year-old daughter. Again, the presence and fear went away, and Colleen slept soundly that night. And just like with the magazines, my casualness toward this sin was over. I started to realize that I could not afford to dabble in getting high ever again. I was through with another pet sin. What an amazing week for changes in my thinking and in my attitude toward my commitment to the Lord.

> *Having experienced my own recent encounter with demonic fear, how could I possibly be so calloused as to ignore my own daughter's plea for help?*

As the days passed, I was becoming aware of an ever-stronger feeling that the Holy Spirit was camping near to me. I found myself having a series of emotional encounters with the Lord where I would repent with tears from a wide range of bad choices that I had made. I was becoming so broken and so grateful that Jesus was even taking me back, that I was effusive in thanking the Lord. I didn't deserve Him. Not only had I squandered away the years of my thirties, but I had ignored the Lord altogether. My life had been filled with a seemingly never ending stream of self-centered thinking and selfish pursuits.

Two Evils to Stay Away From

In Jeremiah, God spoke to Israel through His prophet and said:

> For my people have committed two evils: they have forsaken Me, the fountain of living waters, and hewn themselves cisterns—broken cisterns that can hold no water (Jeremiah 2:13).

Just like Israel, I, too, had drifted away from God and trusted in the things that were about as reliable as a cracked coffee mug. My greatest regret was that I had left Him. I had ignored the One who loved me, the One who called me and used me as a teenager, the One who went to the cross for me, and I had filled my life with things that didn't satisfy me.

In returning to the Lord in 1996, I especially remember two things that happened to me. First, I remember sitting in the service of Bethlehem's First Presbyterian Church that seats 900 and sensing such a deep, gut-wrenching need for the Lord in my life that all I could do was quietly but with great intensity cry out to God with my thoughts. I would tell Him over and over that I needed Him so much. Second, I remember a growing love and deep, deep gratitude for the fact that despite all of my carelessness and backsliding, Jesus had come after me to restore me. I didn't wake up one morning and decide to come back to a right relationship with God. Instead, it was like He tapped me on the shoulder when I wasn't looking. Jesus really is an incredible shepherd, and when the time was right, He approached me and brought me back into His fold.

The next challenge that the Lord began to impress upon me was to use my driving time as my prayer time. Driving to work turned into an awesome slice in the day of rich intimacy. It was a brief opportunity to bask in the sunshine of His presence and soak in His joy. Within a few minutes after seeking Him, a highly noticeable and tangible presence of the Holy Spirit would seem to fill up the cavity of the car's interior. It was the same feelings of liquid love that drew me to His goodness as a boy and as a teenager. These were times when He would reveal to me how much He loved me and that He had plans to use me.

WHAT'S YOUR HEAVENLY FATHER LIKE?

Some people have a distorted view of what God is like. Yes, the Bible tells us that there will be a day of judgment, but what does the Bible tell us about His thinking and intentions toward us right now? I have personally met those who believe that God is not a loving Father but is more like a celestial judge. They will imply that God is mad at them and He will reject them if they try to approach Him. I believe that this is one of the reasons why Jesus gave us the parables of the lost sheep, the lost coin, and the lost son. These parables address many of the distorted views about what God is like and how God the Father will respond to someone who comes back to Him.

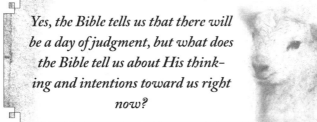

Yes, the Bible tells us that there will be a day of judgment, but what does the Bible tell us about His thinking and intentions toward us right now?

In Luke 15, Jesus addressed a Jewish crowd that needed some insight as to the real nature of a forgiving God. The Pharisees and scribes were complaining that Jesus was not rejecting the sinners and tax collectors the way a religious man should. Jesus responded to them with these three parables. He wanted them to understand what God was really like.

In the parable of the lost sheep, Jesus shares with them that at the very core of God's being, He wants to take extreme measures to secure the return and safety of a lost sheep. When

He finds someone who is lost, Jesus shows us through this parable that the Father is not mad at the individual but incredibly joyful that He has regained a lost sheep. Even the angels join Him in the excitement. In other words, there's a party going on in Heaven every time someone who was away from God becomes found again.

I say to you that likewise there will be more joy in heaven over one sinner who repents than over ninety-nine just persons who need no repentance! (Luke 15:7)

The parable of the lost coin is reinforcement to the parable of the lost sheep. If there are ten silver coins in a set and one is missing, won't there be considerable effort by the owner to find it? And wouldn't the owner become happy and excited when it was found? People are so valuable and important to God that He will always rejoice when someone turns away from his or her wrongdoing and makes steps in His direction.

What is God like? It's as if Jesus answers this question in the parable of the lost son.

Then He [Jesus] *said: "A certain man had two sons, and the younger of them said to his father, 'Father, give me the portion of goods that falls to me.' So he divided to them his livelihood. And not many days after, the younger son gathered all together, journeyed to a far country, and there wasted his possessions with prodigal living. But when he had spent all, there arose a severe famine in that land and*

*he began to be in want. Then he went and joined himself
to a citizen of that country, and he sent him into his fields
to feed swine. And he would gladly have filled his stomach
with the pods that the swine ate and no one gave him anything. But when he came to himself, he said, 'How many of
my father's hired servants have bread enough and to spare,
and I perish with hunger! I will arise and go to my father
and will say to him, 'Father, I have sinned against heaven
and before you, and I am no longer worthy to be called your
son. Make me like one of your hired servants.' And he arose
and came to his father. But when he was still a great way
off his father saw him and had compassion, and ran and
fell on his neck and kissed him. And the son said to him,
'Father, I have sinned against heaven and in your sight
and am no longer worthy to be called your son.' But the
father said to his servants, 'Bring out the best robe and put
it on him, and put a ring on his hand and sandals on his
feet. And bring the fatted calf here and kill it, and let us eat
and be merry; for this my son was dead and is alive again;
he was lost and is found* (Luke 15:11-24).

What was it that mattered to the father in the parable of
the lost son? Was he quick to punish his wayward son or to
reject him? Why is it so typical for people to presume that
God's nature is more anger than love? Jesus is proclaiming in
this story that this is what your heavenly Father is like. With all
your faults and all your straying away, God will come to you as
you take even tentative steps toward Him. And while you are

still a little way off, He will run to meet you. Not only that, but He'll even hug you and kiss your neck with affection. The Lord is looking for you to come over the hill and head in His direction. He's more than ready to forgive you. Even though you may have squandered what He has given you, He will take you back with open arms. Your heavenly Father will put the family ring on your finger, give you His best robe, put new shoes on your feet, feed you the choicest food, and throw a party for you in a celebration that's complete with music and dancing. That's what our God and heavenly Father is like. He loves lost sheep, and He deeply loves you, just like the father in the parable loved his lost son. This is not only sound theology from the Bible, but I happen to know that it's true from personal experience. I was that lost son who became found.

Why is it so typical for people to presume that God's nature is more anger than love?

Points to Ponder

1. In the beginning of Chapter 7, the author writes about coming back to Jesus Christ. Who initiated it, and how did it happen?

_____

_____

_____

2. Can the spiritual choices that you personally make in life have a spiritual impact on your family?

_____

_____

_____

3. According to Jeremiah 2:13, what two evils did Israel commit against the Lord?

_____

_____

_____

4. What can we learn from this passage?

_____

_____

_____

5. Have you ever thought about using your drive time as a prayer and worship time?

_____

_____

_____

6. According to the parable of the lost son in Luke 15, what is your heavenly Father like?

_____

_____

_____

Part Three:

Coming Back to Jesus

Chapter 8

THREE EARLY LESSONS

*D*uring the early months of my comeback in 1996, Nancy and I started attending First Presbyterian Church in Bethlehem. At the time, this church had a membership role of about 3,000, and because their lead pastor, Rev. Keith Brown, and one or two of their other pastors provided rich life application sermons from the Bible, we decided to plug into the life of the church. While I was there for two years, the Lord wanted to teach me three incredible lessons. First, judging others is not my job, but loving others is (see Matt. 7:1)! Second, when it comes to ministry, I've got nothing. There's no spiritual ministry at all without the anointing of the Holy Spirit; and third, when it comes to His work, it's not about me and my services, but it's all about Jesus and the needs of the sheep.

First Presbyterian had a very dynamic youth department, especially their middle school Sunday morning program that they called Prime Time. It was a great blend of fun, a couple of cutting-edge worship songs, and a short object lesson from the Bible by Youth Pastor Eric Kraihanzel. My older daughter Colleen was in the sixth grade, and she loved the program so much that she was always inviting her friends to come with her on Sunday. I decided to plug in as the guy who would lead them in a couple of songs, which took about five minutes. But I took it seriously and would spend time early in the morning praying for Prime Time and asking for God's presence to be felt by the kids and for His Word to penetrate their hearts.

LESSON ONE: JUDGING OTHERS IS NOT MY JOB

After a few months of this, I was asked if I would like to help three other men in teaching the eighth grade boys after the big group would break into smaller groups. Of course I said that I would love to, and for a number of Sundays I would watch the other men take turns teaching. At this point I was pretty much in charge of nothing; yet I was a walking revival, I was head-over-heels in love with Jesus, and I was champing at the proverbial bit to teach or preach or take on anything that they might give me. A couple of times I was asked if I wanted to speak to the kids in the chapel, and each time it was canceled for some reason. I remember saying to my wife that I kept writing sermons that no one would hear. God was testing my attitude. I would find myself perplexed and asking the Lord why He wasn't using me more. "Come on, Lord! I am so ready, and You're not doing anything."

I was wrestling with a superiority complex. Yes, I was going through a kind of spiritual soaking time in my life and I was red hot on fire for the Lord, yet there was this underlying temptation to compare myself to other Christians, especially those who didn't display the same effusive emotions for Jesus as me. With hindsight, I can see that judging the extent of someone else's spirituality is not my God-appointed job. My job is to love others regardless of where they are at spiritually and complete whatever assignments He may give me.

LESSON TWO: I'VE GOT NOTHING

Then one Sunday, George, who had been in charge of the eighth grade boys Sunday school for years, told me that I had the lesson for the next week. I began to talk with George about the fact that many of these eighth grade boys had never turned away from things that displease God or given their lives to Jesus. George began to tell me that these guys, like most teenagers, would probably not get serious about God until they were much older and had families of their own.

Well, this was not my observation in life. Because I was saved as a teenager and I saw literally thousands of young people make decisions for Christ during the Jesus Movement, I decided to lock horns with George and argued my point ad nauseam. When I left our little debate, my prideful thoughts took this conversation about teenage boys accepting Christ, and turned it into a challenge. OK, George, I've got next week's lesson so...game on! I began to pray for those boys every day. I designed a lesson about how to get saved and was going to blast them with great soundbites and pepper it all with lots of Scripture. Why, this could even be the beginnings of revival for the whole church! I envisioned the entire class, with tears pouring down their cheeks, coming to Christ.

That Sunday morning was a complete disaster. Nothing went right. I had technical problems with my soundbites, and there was no tangible presence of anything, except maybe my tangible frustration. I felt like a stand-up-comedian who was bombing on stage and you could see glistening beads of sweat forming on his forehead as he'd loosen his tie for air.

If I was a comedian, I would have heard crickets. I'm pretty sure that when I asked for a decision, all I got was silence and the occasional light cough. When it was all over, I couldn't wait to get out of there, and I left that Sunday school room with my tail between my legs. I realized that without the Holy Spirit, I've got nothing.

Embarrassed and humiliated I left the church campus quickly and found one of my praying spots. It was a corner at the back of the giant supermarket parking lot. I sat in the car and began to ask the Lord about it all. "Lord, what happened there? Where were you? Your hand was completely off me. This must be what it's like to minister in my own strength, because I'll tell You, Lord, it felt like You were a million miles away from me this morning. Dear Lord, why didn't you back me up?" The Holy Spirit took me by surprise by strongly answering me. He impressed upon me that He didn't back me up because I was competing with George, the head of the eighth grade boys' class. My motives were based on pride and wanting to be competitive.

ABIDE IN ME

The "You're competing with George" lesson was one of the hardest lessons that the Lord has ever given me, but it is also one of the richest. It's really two-fold. First comes the obvious. I cannot be motivated by pride or a competitive spirit when ministering for the Lord. Looking back on this, it should have been a no-brainer and should have dropped my competitive spirit. My motivation needs to be love, not winning an argument. And the second lesson is this: I can't do anything useful or productive in ministry without His anointing, without His hand on me. When I spoke that Sunday morning, I was on my own, without any assistance from the Holy Spirit. His hand was off me. Jesus taught His disciples in John 15 that they needed Him in order to be fruitful.

Abide in Me, and I in you. As the branch cannot bear fruit of itself, unless it abides in the vine, neither can you unless you abide in Me. I am the vine, you are the branches. He who abides in Me, and I in him bears much fruit; for without Me you can do nothing (John 15:4-5).

LESSON THREE: IT'S NOT ABOUT ME

After ten weeks of "Inquirer's Class," Nance and I were encouraged to join First Presbyterian Church and commit to a new small group that was forming. This consisted of 12 new people who had joined the church just like we had. The leader was only temporary and was hoping that we would become the facilitators of the group. On the one hand, we felt like the Lord was gently nudging us to become the new leaders, but on the other hand, Nancy and I were not getting much out of it in terms of spiritual enrichment. Those who were in our group came from a wide range of former backgrounds: Roman Catholics, Universalists, lapsed Presbyterians. When we would discuss spiritual things or conduct a Bible study, it became clear that we were not exactly on the same wavelength.

I remember one Bible study when we were discussing everyone's thoughts on the story of Jesus casting out demons in Luke 8:26-39.

Jesus said to the voices coming out of the man, "What is your name?" And he said "Legion, for we are many" and the demons begged Jesus to send them into a herd of feeding swine.

Jesus gave them permission and they entered the herd.

Verse 33 says that the pigs ran violently down a steep slope and into a lake and drowned. And this became the big sticking point for some in our small group. What about the pigs? Why did the pigs have to die? Those poor pigs! I said, "But isn't it great that the man was set free? He's been delivered from demonic forces, right? Isn't that good?"

One woman in our group kept repeating, "Well I don't think this was fair to the pigs!" There were some in our small group who seemed to be more focused on the prevention of cruelty to animals than on seeing someone set free. I also remember someone saying that she didn't really like the idea of going to church more than once a week and she was not comfortable talking about God. Coming home from the pig debate that night, Nance and I agreed that we'd had enough! Our original small group expectations were that we were going to be fed spiritually and have the kind of Christian fellowship that would keep us humming through the next two weeks. We were not getting what we wanted out of it.

Our original small group expectations were that we were going to be fed spiritually and have the kind of Christian fellowship that would keep us humming through the next two weeks. We were not getting what we wanted out of it.

On the night that we were scheming for a way out of this small group, the Lord gave Nancy one of those passages that hits you right between the eyes. Although God had been using us to lead and guide our small group, we were ready to throw in the towel and go find something else that would better feed us spiritually. Here is the passage that Nancy found:

> *Again the word of the Lord came to me, saying, "Son of man, prophesy against the shepherds of Israel, prophesy and say to them, 'Thus says the Lord God to the shepherds: Woe to the shepherds of Israel who feed themselves! Should not the shepherds feed the flocks?'"* (Ezekiel 34:1-2)

We both felt so strongly that the Lord was speaking to our situation, that we were not placed in that small group for our benefit, but for their benefit. In other words, it's not about me! It's about serving Jesus Christ by serving others. This is the metamorphosis that the Lord wants for every follower of Christ. Just as a caterpillar transforms into a butterfly, believers need to eventually stop thinking about their needs all the time and begin thinking about how they can be of service to others. American churches are filled with believers who will join a church only because it has the right programs for their family or it has the best preaching and the best worship in a 50-mile radius. Likewise, Christians will often abandon their support of a church because they're not getting enough out of it; it's too big or it's too small or it doesn't have all the buttons and whistles that they want. Some may leave for immature reasons like, the pastor didn't shake my hand, sister so-and-so offended me ,or somebody keeps sitting in my church seat.

I know of one couple who decided to leave their church family because the church ceilings were too low. The questions we need to ask ourselves are, "How can I serve? Where does God want me to serve?" It may be that the Lord has called you to a big and beautifully functional church, but if the Lord is calling you to serve in a church that's less than perfect, then maybe you're being led into a place where you're needed and you're going to serve, not the other way around. Jesus still loves you if you hold on to a "What about me?" mentality, but what He wants is for consumer sheep to grow up and become producing shepherds. It's the Christian metamorphosis. Jesus is still asking His disciples today the same all-important question that He had once asked Peter: *"Do you love me?...Feed my sheep"* (John 21:17).

> *The questions we need to ask ourselves are, "How can I serve? Where does God want me to serve?"*

Points to Ponder

1. The danger that comes with spiritual pride is the temptation to become critical and judgmental of others. Have you ever struggled with this? Read Luke 18:9-14, which is "The Parable of the Pharisee and the Tax Collector" and discuss.

_____

_____

_____

_____

_____

2. What did Jesus mean when He said, "Without Me you can do nothing" in John 15:5? Can this apply to ministering to others, and if so, how?

_____

_____

_____

_____

_____

3. Is it ever acceptable to be competitive with others in ministry? Why or why not?

_____

_____

_____

_____

4. What do consumer sheep look for when choosing a church?

_____

_____

_____

_____

5. What questions should be asked of the mature, shepherd-minded believer before choosing a church?

_____

_____

_____

Chapter 9

FEELING PREGNANT WITH A CALL

A sense of calling was returning to me and becoming stronger. I felt like I was in a preparation period for greater usefulness. This period seemed like the fine-tuning of a radio station. The coarse tuning was turning my heart away from the frequencies of temptation and worldly thinking. The fine–tuning, however, felt more like a daily classroom designed to teach me obedience to His gentle voice. For example, it's not necessarily a sin to smack your dog on the nose when he relieves himself on the carpeting, but I sensed that the Holy Spirit was putting it on my heart to stop trying to correct my dog this way. It was ironic that when I stopped this practice, the dog only went outdoors.

I also remember watching a pastor on television and I was starting to criticize him before my wife. I immediately sensed a very sharp rebuke from the Holy Spirit that stopped me in mid-sentence. It was a strong impression that the Lord was essentially saying to me, "Don't you dare tear down this servant of Mine who I have called to do my work. He is one of my shepherds." It made a lasting impression on me, and I have since learned to be very careful when it comes to speaking anything that tears down others in ministry. I'm reminded of Proverbs 6:16, *"These six things the Lord hates, Yes seven are an abomination to Him."* What's the seventh thing that God really hates? *One who sows discord among the brethren* (Prov. 6:19).

God hates the other six behaviors in Proverbs 6, but this last one He really hates. Most of our day-to-day differences among other Christians are minor. They are either culturally different or involve nuances in biblical interpretation that have to do with minor or non-essential beliefs. If someone is not involved in scandalous sin or preaching another Gospel, then I need to edit my thoughts and guard my mouth before speaking at all.

More and more, I felt that I was being tested in a variety of ways, but a lot of the testing had to do with the things that could come out of my mouth. If I was going to represent Jesus Christ, I could no longer take a casual approach to colorful joke-telling, gossip, or anything that would be inappropriate for a Christian leader to say. Not that I was anything as of yet, but I was in training for a specific calling. One little trick that helped me immeasurably was a similar exercise to asking the question, "What would Jesus do?" I think that's a great question to ask yourself, but what worked for me was asking the question, "What would Billy Graham say in this situation, or how would Billy Graham respond to this person?" If I couldn't see the words I was going to say coming out of Billy Graham's mouth, then the conclusion was that I shouldn't say it either. This was not to put Billy Graham on a higher pedestal of perfection than others; it was just easier for me to identify with Billy as a role model. These kinds of disciplines and tests went on for almost two years without any specific calling from God.

If I was going to represent Jesus Christ, I could no longer take a casual approach to colorful joke-telling, gossip, or anything that would be inappropriate for a Christian leader to say.

THE CALL TO BE A SHEPHERD

In my prayer time, the Lord impressed upon my heart that I needed to visit Elim in Lima, New York. Elim consisted of three entities on one campus: Elim Fellowship,

Elim Bible Institute, and Elim Gospel Church. In 1998, Elim Fellowship used the facilities of E.B.I. for their summer meetings. I said to my wife, "Honey, how do you feel about going up to Elim?" She told me that God was putting the exact same thing on her heart! In addition to getting this kind of direction to go to Elim, we both felt impressed during prayer that the Lord was going to have a word of direction or maybe a calling to give me at Elim. Several days later, we received a flyer in the mail that Elim's summer camp meeting was going to start on June 28, 1998. We both thought that this would be a good time to go up there with our daughters, attend the meetings, and maybe go for a drive and check out Niagara Falls next to Buffalo, New York.

As a family, we drove up to Lima on a Sunday and went to the meeting that night. We were expecting some kind of ministry or possibly a call to take place. The next day we took our girls onto a tourist boat at Niagara Falls called Maid of the Mist. That night we made it to another Elim meeting, and that's when it actually happened.

A preacher from California named Moses Vegh spoke on being vessels of honor, fit for the Master's use, from Second Timothy 2:20-22. He called everyone to the altar who wanted to renew their vows to Christ and receive a fresh touch from God. At least 100 or more of us came down the aisles and stood around the front podium. There was a powerful sense of God's presence as we sang in worship at the front.

Then Moses Vegh said something that hit me like a ton of bricks. He said, "Some of you were called by the Lord to go into ministry as teenagers, but you've fallen off the potter's wheel, and now God is calling you back into service."

As if that wasn't enough to hear, I experienced a loud, strong, and clear voice resonating on the inside of me. The Lord spoke to me and said, "Haven't I given you a pastor's heart?" There it was—the specific calling into ministry that I had been waiting for my whole life. This was the calling that eluded me in my twenties because I wasn't faithful enough; the calling that left me in my thirties because of my chronic drifting and backsliding. He actually called me! He brought me back and fulfilled the calling that I sensed as a teenager but never had. It was always a general sense of calling that pushed me toward a BA in biblical studies but never anything specific. I never felt totally comfortable launching into full-time ministry just because I earned a degree in it. I needed to be called. I needed this night.

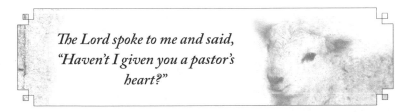

The Lord spoke to me and said, "Haven't I given you a pastor's heart?"

Since my experience on June 29, 1998, I have read about and heard about all the different ways that God can call individuals into ministry. The calling can come as that still, small voice on the inside of you, or it can be as simple as a growing conviction that God wants you to take steps toward an open door of opportunity. However the call comes, it is the prerequisite to being used by God in the specific ministry that He has planned for you to do. Shepherds are called.

THE WAL-MART PRINCIPLE

Have you ever sensed even a vague calling on your life but there's nothing specific? I believe that God is holding off on the specific call until He can determine both faithfulness and readiness. For me, it all began with a general feeling that I was supposed to do more with my life than just occupy a seat on Sunday morning. But what kind of work did God want me to do? Jesus lets us know in no uncertain terms that there is a shortage of workers in God's kingdom. In Matthew 9, Jesus has compassion on the crowds and calls them sheep without a shepherd. Then in verses 37 and 38 He says:

> *The harvest is plentiful but the workers are few. Ask the Lord of the harvest, therefore, to send out workers into his harvest field* (Matthew 9:37-38).

There's a big harvest out there, there's a shortage of workers, and so, it may seem to make sense for some of us to just pick a calling and start working. But that's not what Jesus is telling us to do. We're supposed to ask the Lord to send workers. In the business world, workers always need to be commissioned by the organization that's in charge of the work. If Wal-Mart has a new store opening in your area and there are 45 job openings, people are not allowed by Wal-Mart to just show up and start doing retail work. They have to be screened. Some people, for a variety of reasons, will not be hired. If they filled out an application for employment, it could be found out that they were unfaithful with their former employers or just very unreliable. It could be that the applicant doesn't really want the job or has a bad attitude toward anyone telling him or her what to do. It might be that the potential employee is just too inexperienced to handle a particular job opportunity.

Then there are those Wal-Mart will hire. They get "the call" from Wal-Mart, and they will hear something like "Welcome aboard" or "When can you start?" Then the new hire is put on payroll, but there's a training period before he or she takes on the full responsibility of the job.

My point is that Wal-Mart chooses who will work for them. It is not the decision of the job seekers to determine whether or not they will be put on the job. It is the Lord of the harvest who chooses His workers, and it is He who sends them. Once Wal-Mart screens the individual and he or she passes the application process, it's then that the company decides to call back the job seeker and tell him or her that he or she got the job. Jesus is not asking us in Matthew 9 to go book the next flight to Borneo and start a mission there.

But what He is asking is for us to be aware of all the

work that's out there and to pray that the Lord of the harvest will send or "call up" more usable individuals to be workers in His harvest fields. Hopefully, if you're not called to a ministry yet, you will begin to seek the Lord about becoming one of those usable individuals. Ultimately, any servant of the Lord who is called to shepherd people or go after the lost sheep of this world is appointed and sent into the harvest fields by the Holy Spirit. There's a divine "calling" involved. Every new believer who starts to get serious about the things of God should begin to feel a sense of that general calling on his or her life. The Lord is looking for qualified workers to work in His harvest fields. That sense of general calling is God letting you know that He is extremely interested in your response to Him at this juncture. There's no specific calling yet, but I believe that He is hopeful that you will respond to Him with a deep desire to take that sense of calling to the next level. Why? Because the harvest is plentiful, but the laborers are few.

Getting from that general calling to a specific calling can take a time of preparation. After our first heartfelt commitment of our lives to Jesus Christ, there are often a lot of issues to work out in us before, as it says in Second Timothy 2:21, we become *"...an instrument for noble purposes, made holy, useful to the Master and prepared to do any good work"* (NIV). We can be completely born-again and a sheep in God's fold and yet not be ready or useful for what He has in store for us to do. I had that general calling, that sense that the Lord had plans to use me in specific and useful ways, but my problem was "the yo-yo syndrome" and eventually drifting. Sometimes I was doing great spiritually and sometimes I wasn't.

Sometimes I was living a clean life and I was on fire for the Lord, and sometimes I would return to pet sins. My sticking point with God was that I was not consistent in living for Him. I wasn't solid. I was unpredictable from year to year. I wasn't a consistently clean and holy vessel ready for the Master's use. In other words, in keeping with the Wal-Mart analogy, the Lord was not about to call me for a specific job. I failed the screening process. It wasn't until I was converted again that a sense of God's calling began to rest on me. After a season of purging and testing, mixed with renewed faithfulness and a deep, sustained love for Jesus, the general calling developed into a specific calling. Jesus first called me to Himself, and then He gave me a season of testing and growth. It wasn't until hundreds of right choices were made over an extended period of time that the "other" calling came to fruition.

Points to Ponder

1. Proverbs 6 lists seven sins that the Lord hates. Which one does He hate the most? How can we keep ourselves from doing this behavior?

_____

_____

_____

2. Anyone who wants to become mature and more usable for God's assignments needs to watch his or her words. What did the author do to train his speech?

_____

_____

_____

3. Read James 3:1-5. What does James say about teaching others and the tongue?

_____

_____

_____

4. According to Second Timothy 2:20-22, how can we become vessels of honor and useful to the Master for good works?

_____

_____

_____

5. What is the "Wal-Mart" principle? Explain the process for hiring.

_____

_____

_____

6. How does the "Wal-Mart" principle echo Jesus' words in Matthew 9:38: *"Therefore pray the Lord of the Harvest to send out laborers into His harvest."*

_____

_____

_____

7. How does a general sense of calling become a clear and specific calling from God?

_____

_____

_____

Chapter 10

A TIME TO SHEPHERD

OK, I've heard from God and I've got a call on my life, but now what? Deciding how to proceed was anything but an exact science, so as I prayed and explored possible ways to fulfill the call, God proved faithful over time to always give me direction. My praying went something like this: "Lord, is this what You want me to do?" I would ask Him for clear guidance as I pursued plan A or plan B. I was acknowledging Him in the process of finding God's specific will for me. I believed that He would direct me. In my prayer for direction, I was leaning on the biblical promise found in Proverbs 3:5-6 that if we acknowledge Him as we go forward in every step, then He will direct our path. I would go into this passage more near the end of this chapter.

In my prayer for direction, I was leaning on the biblical promise found in Proverbs 3:5-6 that if we acknowledge Him as we go forward in every step, then He will direct our path.

The first thing that came to my mind was born out of logical thinking. I was asking the Lord for direction, but I was leaning heavily on my own understanding. I received a tri-fold advertisement for Princeton Theological Seminary. This made sense for me on a few levels. I was raised Presbyterian. I was at that time going to First Presbyterian Church of Bethlehem, and after all, I got this really cool flyer in the mail. As I thought about this potential opportunity, I noticed that there were both positives and negatives to it. If accepted, there was a good possibility of receiving a full ride. On the problem side, I had heard that Princeton's theology was more liberal in their approach to the Bible than my core conservative beliefs. Going to Princeton would also take me out of ministry for three years, and Nancy would have to be the sole bread-winner for the family while I pursued a Master's of Divinity degree on campus. In the final analysis, it never came down to a ledger listing the positive reasons in one column and listing the negative reasons in the other column but an awareness of God's will for me. Every time

I prayed about it, there was something inside of me saying, "No, you are not going to go this way." If I took any steps in pursuing seminary at Princeton, I would lose my peace of mind. This just wasn't God's plan for me.

On the other hand, I had remembered that Elim Fellowship would recognize my educational background and might possibly give me a "license to minister." This time when I prayed about it, I sensed God's presence and approval. In every little step I took toward getting the license, I felt His blessings of peace and joy. Being in community with Elim Fellowship also gave me a board to which I was accountable. I remember seeking the Lord for direction in my basement one day, when I felt His presence come on me so strongly that I was compelled to get on my knees and elbows for a long time. As God's presence continued to intensify, I heard the Lord speaking on the inside of me that He wanted me to plant a church. I was so grateful that He was giving me direction, but it also presented a whole new set of potential problems. How do I do that? I'll need a core group to help me. Where do I plant a church and how do I begin? It was an unfolding process.

I put an ad in the newspaper that said that I was going to start a church and if anyone was interested, then they could meet me in the Hamilton Inn conference room in Bethlehem. That meeting produced about seven people. We met for several months, and just before Easter I mailed a

7,000-piece flyer to new people in the area, which produced about 35 on Easter Sunday. We met in a karate studio, and for one year I was the pastor of a small church plant called Greater Harvest. I learned a lot about the realities of ministry and the difficulties that come with shepherding people and trying to grow a new church. Because we were meeting in a karate studio, I had problems with some of the kids who would find the nunchucks and would swing them over their heads while chasing each other around in circles. If people came in the front door, they had to walk through an indoor miniature golf course, and another door set off an alarm to the police department. The police were less than happy with us because they had to come out to our little church plant Sunday after Sunday and turn the alarm off. I experienced a power struggle with my new worship leader, out-of-control kids in our children's church, and a few spouses who would seek counseling because of cyberspace infidelity (chat room relationships). My church planting days were difficult, but they also stretched me and gave me enough experience to step into another ministry that brought about hundreds of salvations.

There was an opening for a senior pastor at a church that I'll call Northeast Baptist Church (NBC). NBC was formally Southern Baptist, and so was their retiring pastor. As I was praying about this, I later told my wife that this opportunity felt like God was in it. After running off my resume and creating a cover letter, Nance and I held the paperwork up to the Lord in our kitchen, and as we prayed, it felt like we were spiritually shot through with a bolt of electricity. We stood there amazed and awestruck by the power of God's presence on us. Nance and I looked at each other, and we both said at the same time that this was going to happen!

Months went by, and we didn't hear anything from NBC. We started to doubt our experience in the kitchen that day. Honey, what was that? Was it me, was it God, or was it the pizza we had? Why haven't we heard anything? About one week later, I received a phone call from NBC, and they needed a guest speaker on short notice. That began an amazing process that lifted me above the crowd of the other 300 or so applicants. I was given several more opportunities to preach, and they started the interview process. I had very little experience at the time, but because of the favor of the Lord, things went very smoothly. I was installed in October of 2000, and I quit my day job to pastor a church of around 120.

WHICH WAY DO I GO?

Any calling to shepherd should be followed by receiving some direction. The question is no longer, "Am I called?" but it becomes, "Which way do I go?" Please humor me by letting me state the obvious. Those who need direction need to spend time in prayer and ask God for guidance from the Holy Spirit. And I'm not talking about a five-minute session where you ask for direction like you ask for God's blessing on your chicken dinner. "Lord bless me with your guidance, amen." Even Jesus would go and find a quiet place before dawn and commune with His Father in order to hear what the game plan was. The church at Antioch practiced this kind of praying in Acts 13, and it resulted in divine direction for Barnabas and Saul (Paul).

> *As they ministered to the Lord and fasted, the Holy Spirit said, "Now separate to Me Barnabas and Saul for the work to which I have called them"* (Acts 13:2).

Jesus tells us in Matthew 7:7, *"Ask and it will be given to you, seek and you will find; knock and it will be opened"*. We should always ask the Lord, "Which way do I go?"

GETTING DIRECTION

Realistically, when you go to prayer asking God for guidance, you will probably not get a voice from above giving you GPS-like directions. Even if you did get a strong thought, it isn't necessarily a slam-dunk that this is coming from the Holy Spirit. Thoughts that come from our own desires can sometimes be misunderstood as divine guidance. When I was 17, I was dating a Christian girl, and I had it in my head that it would be great to get married. I asked the Lord if I should propose to her. When I turned on the car radio, I heard someone talking about marriage, and I took it as a sign from above that I was supposed to pop the question and we were going to get married. Not only was I broke, too young, and had no visible means of support, but with hindsight, I found out that her motive for marriage was to get away from her parents. Marrying her would have been a recipe for disaster! In addition to the dangers of pursuing your own understanding, it is also possible to hear deceptive thoughts from the enemy. Anytime ministry is about to be launched, the enemy will try to derail it.

So how in the world do we navigate in the waters of divine guidance and direction? There is a teaching on guidance that has been around for a long time. F.B. Meyer, a contemporary of evangelist D.L. Moody, once said this: "When we want to know God's will, there are three things which always occur; the inward impulse, the Word of God and the trend of circumstances...Never act until these three things agree."

Meyer received this insight while standing on the bridge of a ship during a stormy night with low visibility. He asked the captain how he knew when and where to turn his ship into the upcoming narrow harbor. The captain replied, "Do you see those three red lights on the shore? When they are all in a straight line, then I go right in." When the three harbor lights line up, then it's safe to go forward. The inward impulse, which is your impulse from the Holy Spirit, is your first harbor light. Next, your idea for direction has to be in agreement with your second harbor light, the written Word

of God. Finally, the third harbor light to line up is your circumstances. Sometimes moving forward is just a matter of
God's timing, and at the right time, circumstances will align
themselves with the other two harbor lights.

God Will Direct Your Paths

The biblical promise found in Proverbs 3:5-6 is a great
passage to use when seeking God's direction.

*Trust in the Lord with all your heart, and lean not on
your own understanding; in all your ways acknowledge
Him and He shall direct your paths.*

After I've prayed and I see that my harbor lights are in
a straight line, I will then acknowledge the Lord with every
little step that I take. I'll say, "Lord, I'm sending my resume,"
or "Lord, I'm about to go forward with this new program for
the church." Whatever it is that I am progressing toward, I
want to acknowledge and know that because of Proverbs 3:5
and 6, the Lord through His Word is promising to guide
me and to direct my path. God is honored when He is included in the details of our plans, and He is blessed by our
acknowledgment of Him.

Points to Ponder

1. What promise from God is found in Proverbs 3:5-6? How can a believer appropriate this promise and get direction for his or her life?

_____

_____

_____

2. F. B. Meyer explained how he used three harbors lights to line up before proceeding forward; what are they?

_____

_____

_____

3. If your plans are in agreement with the Bible and you have an inner peace from the Holy Spirit, then what might cause a delay in your plans?

_____

_____

_____

4. Can Christians use both instructions (Proverbs 3:5 and the harbor light teaching) to help them understand when to move forward?

_____

_____

_____

Part Four:

Becoming a Shepherd

Chapter 11

REVIVAL IN BETHLEHEM

When I started as the new pastor for Northeast Baptist Church, I was immediately drawn to participate and oversee the Wednesday night prayer meeting at the church. In the fall of 2000, we developed a list of ten prayer points. We then put them on a poster and called it "Prayer Push 2001." At the top of the poster was prayer request number one, that God would send us a revival. We were asking that He would send fire and renewal to NBC. The second item on the list was that NBC would see at least 100 people give their lives to Jesus Christ in 2001. Every Wednesday night, we pleaded for God to send us a revival and that at least 100 "lost sheep" would be found in 2001. Our prayer group had no programs or game plan other than to make sure that we prayed for revival faithfully and for the items on that list. As early as January of 2001, we began to keep track of a person here and a person there being led to Christ through one-on-one evangelism or answers to altar calls at Sunday services, baptisms, and funerals. By May of 2001, our list was up to about 53 decisions for Christ. Church attendance was increasing, and the overflow wing of the church was just as full on Sunday as the main sanctuary. God's presence was becoming stronger Sunday by Sunday, and there was an excitement in the air.

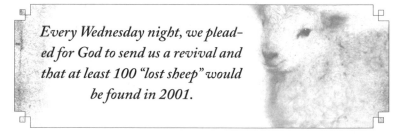

Every Wednesday night, we pleaded for God to send us a revival and that at least 100 "lost sheep" would be found in 2001.

Earlier in the year, I was praying and I received such a powerful impression from the Lord that I wrote it down on paper and kept it on my dresser so that I could refer to it and not forget it. I wrote on a small piece of paper, "We have to do this! *Heaven's Gates, Hell's Flames.*" This was a play that I had heard about, and I heard that it was a powerful tool to win the lost for Christ. The idea of doing this play had just moved from the back burner of ideas to the front burner. I pitched it before the church board, and after some initial resistance, we went forward and secured the date of June 3, 2001, to do three nights of performances. My wife, Nancy, was in charge of keeping the project moving forward and was the liaison between NBC and Reality Outreach Ministries, the organization that promotes and implements this production.

As part of the preparation for the play *Heaven's Gates, Hell's Flames,* many at NBC made a list of friends and loved ones they were planning to invite. We used three Saturday mornings to pray hard for them, and this was in addition to praying for revival and salvations on Wednesday nights. Craig and Lisa Canning came from Reality Outreach Ministries and covered the front of our sanctuary in Mylar (a metallic foil), set up the lighting and sound, and turned much of the congregation into a cast and crew. With a minimal number of rehearsals, we were ready to share the love of Christ and the need to get saved through short scenarios. Typically these scenarios were dramas showing individuals or groups of people facing death by car crash, airplane crash, overdose, or heart attack. With each episode, our church actors found themselves at the gates of Heaven surrounded by silver, gold, and angels. The characters in the play were invited into Heaven or sent away to hell based on whether their names were found in the book of life, and whether they had believed on Jesus during their lifetime.

PENTECOST SUNDAY

On the morning of June 3, 2001, Pentecost Sunday, the church was packed and the front of the sanctuary was covered in silver and gold material in preparation for the drama. It began like any other Sunday morning service, but somewhere in the middle of the worship set, the presence of God became so strong that everyone in the church just froze. Everyone felt such a powerful presence of God that nobody dared to move a muscle or say a word. The music stopped, and there was a holy silence that hung in the air. This silence lasted for a long time, and it felt like we were suspended somehow in eternity between Heaven and earth. God was in the room. The Holy Spirit's presence was so strong that it just filled everything, and then I heard someone in the back begin to quietly weep. Soon there were a dozen or more who started to cry softly. In no time at all, we were all collectively weeping for our friends and family who were spiritually lost and without salvation. The Sunday service liturgy went right out the window, and the service went much longer than planned. It was an awesome experience, and no one wanted to leave. But this particular Sunday, a lot of us needed to get ready for one last afternoon rehearsal before the opening night of *Heaven's Gates, Hell's Flames*.

The Holy Spirit's presence was so strong that it just filled everything, and then I heard someone in the back begin to quietly weep.

The tickets and invitations had gone out, and soon we were watching our church begin to fill up with outsiders. It was still light outside as our members directed cars and ushered people to their seats. In anticipation of new people making a decision to believe in Jesus, we had about 30 Bibles to give out for the three days of the play. When we saw that over 50 people came forward to receive Christ on that first night, we knew that our expectations of what God was going to do were way too small. We had to extend the play to four nights, and on the fourth night we had standing room only. This fourth night, by the way, had been put on without any public advertising. It all spread by word of mouth. It was so crowded that it was a fire marshal's nightmare. We also had to rig a video feed into the church basement to accommodate all the overflow attendees who couldn't fit upstairs in the main sanctuary or "normal" overflow room. For such a small church, we had experienced in four nights well over 200 decisions for Christ in four days. Every decision card got a follow up phone call, and an invitation was extended to come to a discipleship class the following Sunday and a party bash for Jesus, which was going to be held after the evening service.

A SEASON OF SALVATIONS

This play was just the beginning of a season of salvations for us as a church. Lasting about three months, everything that we touched resulted in people getting right with God. We had invited families to come to our grand finale night for Vacation Bible School, and we saw 42 decisions for Christ from the friends and family members of the children. Sunday services, funerals, and any kind of outreach resulted in people raising their hands to get saved. I remember speaking at funerals that summer where a dozen or more would accept the invitation to receive Christ. By the end of the summer of 2001, there were over 500 decisions to receive Jesus Christ as Lord and Savior.

God had blessed our prayers for revival, and a holy breeze had touched hundreds of lost and backsliding sheep that summer. I can't help but wonder what would have happened if I had resisted Him on that incredible day in 1996 when He came to me in the kitchen and called me back to Himself.

FIRESTORM AT NBC

We were warned by the Cannings, from Reality Outreach Ministries, that almost always, in the wake of so many salvations, all hell will break loose in the form of spiritual warfare and demonic backlash. Churches can split, marriages can break up, and the enemy will try to crush any pastor, any church, and any move of the Holy Spirit that has brought about a river of salvations.

We were warned by the Cannings, from Reality Outreach Ministries, that almost always, in the wake of so many salvations, all hell will break loose in the form of spiritual warfare and demonic backlash.

I took this warning to heart and even preached a little bit about how Northeast Baptist needed to brace itself for a wave of warfare. What I didn't realize at the time was that satan will often wait and plot his schemes. He takes his time and looks for opportunities to wreak havoc. It wasn't immediate, but the backlash actually took a few months to marinate. He schemes to start a small fire here and then a small fire there. He looks for weaknesses in individuals. His mode of operation is to get them strongly offended through misunderstandings, half-truths, and complete lies. He works on people's fears, which can often bring about their need to control things. Instead of love, it's fear and the need to take control that become the driving force. When the enemy's schemes are fully developed, then the result will often be a church firestorm.

At Northeast Baptist, things were stirred up to the point of no return. There was a split in the church board and a growing split in the church itself. I remember my wife coming to me with tears in her eyes and saying that she wished that I could just return to the industrial supply business. It's not my intent to go back into all the gritty details of what happened, the church politics and the pain that comes with being in a church firestorm, but suffice to say that sometimes this is the price tag for hosting a revival. It wasn't until after 3,000 were saved on Pentecost in Acts 2, that the persecutions came.

AFTER GLOW

In between the turmoil and my resignation, I was getting letters, emails, and phone calls from people who were expressing how grateful they were that revival had come to us in 2001 and that their loved ones were now following Christ. Whole families were saved that summer, and many were set free from drugs, alcohol, hopelessness, and some from suicidal tendencies. I remember when one older man called me and thanked the Lord that he got saved at NBC. He said that he had terminal cancer and was now ready to spend eternity in Heaven. These ripples of revival had reached far and wide, touching people's lives in Bethlehem, Whitehall, Allentown, Easton, and over the Delaware River into New Jersey. We had asked God for revival, and He sent us one. We had asked the Lord for 100 decisions in 2001, and he gave us a harvest of over 500 who had asked Jesus for forgiveness and a new life in Christ.

THE HARVEST IS ALREADY WHITE

Jesus said to them, "My food is to do the will of Him who sent Me and to finish His work. Do you not say, 'There are still four months and then comes the harvest?' Behold, I say to you, lift up your eyes and look at the fields, for they are already white for the harvest!" (John 4:34-35)

Jesus is telling His disciples that there is a harvest, a massive amount of work to be done out there. Jesus' whole harvest metaphor in John 4:35-36 is about reaching the lost, which is one of the major tasks of shepherding. Going back to Chapter 1, Zechariah 11:16 gave us five responsibilities of shepherding. The first task of shepherding is to bring home the lost sheep. The work of a shepherd will always be in partnership with the Holy Spirit, and that is especially true when it comes to bringing home the lost through evangelism and revival. In the case of the revival at Bethlehem, it was imperative that we sowed in prayer before we reaped a harvest. It was the Holy Spirit who gave us specific direction as to how we should pray and what we should do. It was also the work of the Spirit that led us all to weep for the lost, and it was the Holy Spirit who used the Gospel message to lead so many people to Jesus Christ in such a short amount of time. Shepherding will always be in concert with the work of the Holy Spirit, and an important part of His work is to go after the lost and rescue them.

> *The work of a shepherd will always be in partnership with the Holy Spirit, and that is especially true when it comes to bringing home the lost through evangelism and revival.*

Points to Ponder

1. NBC committed to praying for revival before it actually came. How important is praying for the lost prior to re-vival coming? What specific things were done at NBC to target lost souls?

_____

_____

_____

2. How did God answer NBC's prayer for revival and 100 decisions for Christ?

_____

_____

_____

3. Read Acts 1:4-14. What was it that Jesus told His dis-ciples to do prior to the day of Pentecost?

_____

_____

_____

4. What can happen to the order of a church service when there is an outpouring of the Holy Spirit? What happened at NBC on Pentecost Sunday?

_____

_____

_____

5. How will satan attack a church that is experiencing salvations, healings, and renewal? How can we prepare ourselves to fight these attacks?

_____

_____

_____

6. Which of the five responsibilities of shepherding found in Zechariah 11:16 are fulfilled during a revival?

_____

_____

_____

Chapter 12

A KITCHEN ENCOUNTER

*I*t was a normal day for me as I flipped through a new issue of *Charisma* magazine in the kitchen and sipped my morning coffee. I suddenly took notice of a little one page article about famine coming to the African country of Malawi in 2003. Clive Calver, who had been the president of World Relief International, was quoted as saying that in six months' time, millions could be facing starvation. As I read and re-read the article, I became overwhelmed with a deep compassion for the people of Malawi. It felt like the Holy Spirit was tapping me on the shoulder and saying to me, "Rick, I want you to do something about this." Could this be a new assignment from God? His presence was all around me. But what could I possibly do to help? I wasn't even sure where Malawi was on a map! There was only one thing, just one message that kept replaying over and over again in my mind, like a McDonald's jingle; I had to do something about the coming famine in Malawi, Africa.

So now what? The more that I prayed about it, the more convinced I became that I was supposed to do this. The magazine article said that the world relief efforts were being conducted in the north of Malawi, and as I prayed, I strongly sensed that I was to go to the south. But how was I going to raise that kind of money? Do I buy the food in Africa or do I just ship it over? Where will I get trucks and a crew? How will I know specifically where to go when the time comes and who can help me? I had a hundred questions for God and very few answers. All I knew was that I had to take on this assignment by faith and that eventually I'd have all my questions answered. I could hardly believe that God wanted to send me to one of the poorest nations on the face of this earth with the mission to ease their suffering with food relief and to share the love of Jesus.

Not having a clue as to what I was doing, I set a date to go, and I began to raise money. My hope was that as I stepped out in faith, the Lord would eventually fill in the blanks and unfold the details to me later on. At this juncture I had started a church in Allentown called Living Word Church, and our Sunday services were at the Ramada Inn.

I took a large coffee can, cut a slot in the top, wrapped it in red construction paper that said, "Malawi Famine Relief," and stood before my congregation with it. I said, "Send your pastor to Malawi, Africa!" Unfortunately, this announcement was received with mixed reviews. Some church members thought that this was a crazy thing to do and even encouraged others to not support the pastor in this half-baked project of his. But others decided to donate, and they were excited about being a part of a global outreach where humanitarian aid would be coupled with the preaching of the Gospel. Coffee cans were distributed to other churches as well, and between December of 2002 and March of 2003, we were able to raise a little over $7,000 toward famine relief.

During this fundraising period, the Lord was faithful to give me a lot of answers to all those questions that were puzzling me. Driving up to Elim Bible Institute, I had asked the Lord if He could put me in front of someone who knew a lot about Africa. My daughter Colleen and her friend, Rachel, wanted to visit Elim, and so after five hours of driving through New York, we parked by the cafeteria and went in. As we sat down for lunch, Paul Johannson, the former president of Elim Bible Institute and seasoned missionary to Africa, sat across from me. Paul shared with me some insights into African culture and remembered the time that he and his wife Gloria had invited Maasi tribesmen over for spaghetti and the tribesmen believed that the pasta on their plate were worms. I then asked him if Elim had any missionaries in Malawi and he said no, but he knew that the Assemblies of God denomination had a few there.

After returning home, I called the Assemblies of God headquarters in Springfield, Missouri, and asked for the head of the missions department. When the head of their missions found out that I wanted to distribute food, he said, "Oh, you need the Canadians! Why don't you call this brother in Texas? He's on leave right now, and he's in charge of African missions for the Pentecostal Assemblies of Canada." So I called Texas, and this brother gave me a phone number to call in Malawi, Africa. I called this number and I immediately got in touch with missionaries Arn and Elsie Bowler. I explained to Arn what I wanted to do, and he answered question after question. Through this very special phone call, God was putting together all the pieces of the puzzle for me. Arn finally told me that he could pick me up at the airport in Lilongwe, Malawi, and that I could use his missionary home as a launching pad for my operation. It was Arn and Elsie who helped me to connect with the local African churches, set me up with a crew and vehicles, showed me where to buy food by the ton, and helped me with the exchange rate for converting American dollars into Malawi kwacha. Two very dear Canadian missionaries became God's provision and blessing to me.

Going to Africa

Just eight months after getting a divine directive to feed the poor in Malawi, Africa, I was actually boarding a South African Airbus at JFK airport in New York. Sixteen hours later, I arrived in Johannesburg, South Africa, and called Arn because I wanted to make sure that he had the correct arrival time and flight number for the Malawi leg of the trip. I was making sure that he wouldn't get mixed-up in the Lilongwe International Airport. After a good laugh, Arn told me not to worry too much about flight mix-ups. My flight was the only one coming in that day.

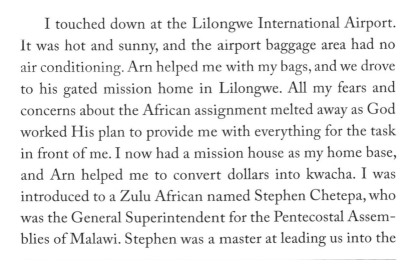

Just eight months after getting a divine directive to feed the poor in Malawi, Africa, I was actually boarding a South African Airbus at JFK airport in New York.

I touched down at the Lilongwe International Airport. It was hot and sunny, and the airport baggage area had no air conditioning. Arn helped me with my bags, and we drove to his gated mission home in Lilongwe. All my fears and concerns about the African assignment melted away as God worked His plan to provide me with everything for the task in front of me. I now had a mission house as my home base, and Arn helped me to convert dollars into kwacha. I was introduced to a Zulu African named Stephen Chetepa, who was the General Superintendent for the Pentecostal Assemblies of Malawi. Stephen was a master at leading us into the south of Malawi, the home of the Shire River Valley and where famine was becoming life-threatening. From local African churches we had gained a crew of seven. I was given the honor of preaching in a local African church on Sunday, and on Monday morning we loaded the big yellow truck and attached trailer with over 20 tons of corn maize and bags of soybeans.

We headed south on the M1 highway toward Blantyre. Up to this point the roads were adequate and our sports utility vehicle played tag with the food truck and its crew. We didn't stop until we reached a rural village near an elephant marsh called Chickwawa. At Chickwawa, we pulled into a walled and gated compound where I was about to experience my first truly African hotel. These are the hotels that are used by traveling locals; they're not designed to accommodate spoiled Americans or Europeans. The teakwood door to my room had wide gaps on the top and bottom, and the door had to be opened or locked with a nineteenth-century skeleton key! The main room was about ten feet by twelve feet, with a small bed and a mosquito net wrapped into a ball and hanging over the pillow. The room included a small wood table and one plastic chair. There was no phone and no television, and the room smelled like Doom, an African bug killer. The walls, the floors, and the ceiling were all made of cement, and I could smell the chemicals of Doom mixed with the stuffiness of the warm night air.

I remember trying to sleep with the light on when I heard the crack of a large flying bug that flew into the wall across from me. As I peered through the holes in my mosquito netting, I saw that this bug had to be the size of a sausage link. Somehow I did manage to get some sleep, and I was ready in the morning for a big day. I decided not to shower in the morning because the shower head was directly over the toilet and there were no hot and cold knobs, just one toggle for on and off. Mosquitoes were everywhere, so I decided to pour bottled water on my head and use a few wipes for my arms and legs. After eating two eggs cooked in grease, bread, and coffee, we prayed as a group and headed south on dirt roads into the Shire River Valley.

Over the next two days, we were able to feed the hungry and malnourished in 12 different villages. At almost every village we came to, children would run along the side of the dusty road shouting "Muzungu," which, loosely translated, means "white person." Stephen Chetepa had set it up for the local pastor in each village to wait for our arrival, along with 10-20 singers. Some would create rhythms, shaking old coffee cans full of pebbles and rocks. At each village we would stack a few hundred ten-kilogram bags of corn maize, preach about the love of Jesus to the crowd, ask them for a decision to receive Christ, and then get the families to line up for the food distribution.

In two days, we were able to feed approximately 5,000 people. Two of the villages were so desperate for food that the orderly lines for food disintegrated into an intense riot over the food bags. All the fighting and shoving was motivated by hunger and need. After preaching six times a day for two days, the Lord blessed us with the joy of watching over 900 Malawians raise their hands to accept Jesus Christ as their Lord and Savior.

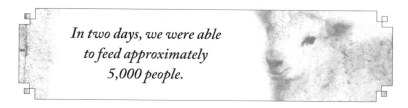

In two days, we were able to feed approximately 5,000 people.

This mission to Malawi was, at times, emotionally overwhelming. We were feeding some of the poorest people on Earth. Many of them wore rags and owned nothing but what they were wearing. Children were taking care of children, and the elderly were taking care of infants because many of their parents had died from AIDS.

The famine of 2003 was caused by mostly drought. When the crops had failed this time, some Africans had resorted to cooking and eating the dried husks of the corn plants—no ears with grain, just crumbled corn husks boiled in water. Stephen Chetepa told me that some were even eating grass to fill their empty bellies.

I thank God that He called on me to do something that was on His heart: feed the poor in Malawi who were in danger of starvation and at the same time, tell them about the good news of Jesus' love. The Lord had it in mind to take care of the remote and forgotten sheep of the Shire River Valley in southern Malawi. And He did it in a holistic way by caring for their physical needs, as well as their spiritual.

SHEPHERDING IS HOLISTIC

What shepherd or sheep farmer doesn't consider the sheep's problems and take action on the most urgent needs? A good shepherd will try to take care of the sheep holistically and at their greatest point of need. In His three years of ministry, Jesus always managed to blend His preaching with taking care of physical needs. In Matthew 14, Jesus had compassion on the 5,000 who were following Him. He healed their sick, fed them a high-protein dinner, and gave them the best spiritual teachings they ever had. Jesus loves people, and He wants His shepherds to lead people spiritually but also to help them at their point of need. These two things go together like peanut butter and jelly. We are supposed to help others holistically so that the love of Christ can be something visible and tangible to them.

When it comes to the marriage of caring for physical needs and spiritual needs, there should be a balance between the two. Both kinds of ministries work best when they are coupled with each other. Teaching and preaching have the greatest penetration into a person's heart when people perceive that the one doing the spiritual feeding also cares about them. God's love is holistic. And at the other end of the ministry spectrum, social services without being tethered somehow to evangelism and reconciliation to God will help people and their immediate needs but will ultimately leave them spiritually lost and without a shepherd. Shepherd work needs to be about helping the whole person get his or her daily bread if he or she is hungry, and his or her fill of Jesus, the Bread of Life.

Points to Ponder

1. What assignment did the author receive from the Lord in his kitchen? What were some of the missing details that he had to work out?

_____

_____

_____

_____

_____

2. When God gives us an assignment, there are often those who will resist us or oppose the project. Did the author get any resistance? How do we stay strong when there are those who want us to ignore what God has put on our heart to do?

_____

_____

_____

_____

_____

3. How did God put all the pieces of the puzzle together for the author? How important were these details in terms of carrying out the assignment?

_____

_____

_____

_____

_____

4. If the Lord put it on your heart to help a group of people who were in desperate need of physical and spiritual assistance, would you do it?

_____

_____

_____

_____

_____

Chapter 13

MALAWI, KENYA, UGANDA

After my first trip to Malawi, Nancy and I started a nonprofit called Bread of Life International. As I prayed about 2004 and kept track of the famine warnings, I felt that I needed to go back to Malawi and do it again. Raising money for feeding the poor in Africa took us in a completely new direction this time. In the summer of 2003, I had met evangelist and pastor Steve Hill, and so I called him on the phone in order to get advice on fundraising. More specifically I wanted to find out how to maybe pitch this on television. Steve was kind enough to suggest that I call Daystar Television Network. It took awhile, but after a number of emails and some phone calls, I was invited to be a guest on a television show called *Celebration* hosted by Marcus and Joni Lamb.

I thank God for Daystar and the opportunity to speak about the needs of Africa to such a large audience. Not only were we able to raise the money needed for the 2004 trip to Malawi, but the Lord connected me with an evangelist in California who wanted to meet me over there. He had seen me on the show, and after a few phone conversations it became clear to me that Don McCardell and I were on the same page.

Don was made for ministry work in Africa, and I had gained a co-laborer in Christ. He was not only able to film the famine relief work, but we were able to split the grueling schedule of preaching 12 or more times in a couple of days. He has a unique affinity for connecting with the poor in Africa and has a gift and a passion for explaining the Gospel in easy to swallow, bite-size pieces. Like a gift from Heaven, he has been meeting me in Africa ever since, and he has become a close friend of mine.

MALAWI AND THE FAMINE OF 2005

The BBC had reported that in 2005 Malawian President Mutharika had declared a national disaster due to food shortages that would threaten up to five million with starvation. As I read the news reports from various sources, it was becoming clear to me that the food distribution in Malawi this time was going to be a "rescue" mission. Malawi's situation had escalated to new levels of concern, and reports were beginning to come in of hunger-related deaths. As bad as things were in 2003 and 2004, this year was going to be something I had yet to experience.

My daughter Patty, who was 15 at the time, had raised most of the money she needed for her own plane ticket to Africa and didn't seem to mind flying out with me on her 16th birthday. We landed in Lilongwe and connected with Arn and Elsie's replacements, Junior and Ivy. Don McCardell arrived the next day all the way from California. In 2005, we had raised enough money to buy over 21 tons of food for the mission. Steve Chetepa soon joined us at the Canadian Mission house, and we began to pray and strategize where to distribute the food this time. Once again we were heading south, but to areas that were especially bad this year.

We were approximately 400 miles south of Malawi's capital city of Lilongwe, and we saw with our own eyes how desperate things were. Because of the lack of rain, our vehicles kicked up huge clouds of reddish dust as we traveled on dirt roads. At our first stop, there were no singing groups to welcome us, just desperate people. We saw the signs of malnutrition and famine: children with bloated bellies, reddish hair, bald patches, and thin arms. At every stop over the next two days, rioting broke out over the food. The fighting was intense but not malicious. I didn't see them trying to hurt each other, but I saw that their objective was to take home a food bag at all costs. It really rocks your soul to see people this hungry.

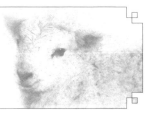

*We saw the signs of malnutrition
and famine: children with bloated
bellies, reddish hair, bald patches,
and thin arms.*

Patty, on more than one occasion, would stay close to the SUV in order to hand out raisin packs, bread rolls and clothing to the children. It would always start out OK, but the children would grow in number quickly, and Patty would see a sea of out-stretched hands reaching toward her face. They pressed her against the Land Rover, and whenever this would happen we would have to get her out of there, out of the crowds of children.

On this particular trip the hunger seemed extreme and preaching the Gospel became, at times, an exercise in futility. They were helplessly distracted by our food truck. On our last village visit before returning to Lilongwe, I saw that the crowd was over a thousand, and I sensed that we were about to be overrun. I yelled up to the truck owner and shouted, "Musa, they're going to overrun the truck." Patty was with others in the SUV, so I climbed up, and the four of us quickly emptied the truck by tossing the remaining bags into the crowd and quickly driving off.

I have never seen such a desperate need for food in all my life. In the famine of 2005 we were able to give out 21 tons of food. We gave out clothes to the threadbare and naked, and we preached when we could. My greatest desire was that we might have had more workers and more trucks full of food that year.

KENYA

Late in 2005, I was monitoring the food situation in Africa and I noticed two things: first, that Malawi was about to have a bumper crop in 2006, and second, a severe drought in the horn of Africa was killing livestock and bringing famine conditions to places like northern Kenya. I began to work the phones and started a relationship by email with Bishop Andrew in Kenya. He became my new contact, and over the next few months we exchanged emails and worked out some of the details.

This time my other daughter, Colleen, wanted to fly with me to Africa. She was a junior at Liberty University and had raised money for her plane ticket by a letter campaign to friends and relatives. Don wasn't able to join me in Kenya that year because he was getting married.

After 16 hours of flying, Colleen and I landed in Nairobi, Kenya, and we were picked up by Bishop Andrew and taken to our hotel. The very next day we met in the hotel lobby, where I ordered coffee and unfolded my big map of Kenya over the coffee table. Bishop Andrew was indispensible as a partner because he was able to secure a truck and knew Kenya. He knew where to get the food, he provided a crew, he knew where the need was the greatest, and he came along with his son Bernard into the famine areas of the north.

After loading the truck with 90-kilogram bags of corn and red beans, we continued north and didn't stop until we came to the Muslim city of Isiolo. Colleen and I checked into a hotel room that had two beds and cement walls with no windows to the outside. It was a little bit claustrophobic, and you could occasionally hear voices in African dialect bouncing off the cement walls and stairs. Adding to our culture shock was the fact that our hotel was right next to a mosque, and so we could hear loud and clear the call to prayer being chanted over the cheap public address system. Listening to the sounds of the mosque reminded me that I was going to preach the next day to a Muslim crowd. I was a little nervous but not enough to change our plans.

The next day we had a crowd of about 300 locals come out to get food. Many of them were women and young girls who had their heads covered according to Muslim traditions. I welcomed them and preached for about 20 minutes on the parable of the lost son. I shared that Jesus wants you to know what God the Father is like and that God is love. He is forgiving and He wants to have a relationship with you. I went on to explain that Christ died for their sins and rose again on the third day. When I asked them to pray in Jesus' name for forgiveness and to invite Christ to be their

Lord and Savior, about 30 people put their hands in the air. I was so blessed to see that kind of response. We gave them all food, and the believers were introduced to the local pastor in Isiolo.

I shared that Jesus wants you to know what God the Father is like and that God is love. He is forgiving and He wants to have a relationship with you.

By early afternoon, we drove further north, all the way to Archer's Post, and we preached and gave out food to over 1,000 hungry Africans from the Samburu tribe. This tribe, like the Maasi tribe, will loop a hole in their ear lobes and stretch them until they hang from their ears like a loose rope. The women wore colorful beads and clothing of brilliant yellow orange. Some of the men were carrying spears or bows and arrows. I'm not sure how many made a decision for Christ because I was inside a meeting place made of grass walls and there were more people outside the grass-covered building listening than inside.

We then traveled into the night to the city of Wamba. Because we arrived at night, the biggest problem for us was to find a safe place to spend the night. We prayed about it, and Bernard drove us to a World Vision compound whose gate guard carried an AK-47. The gate guard turned us away. Our next stop was a high-walled Catholic compound. Two old Italian priests were kind enough to take us in and feed us breakfast in the morning.

The next day was Sunday, and so I preached in the local Wamba church. Afterward the church helped us to set up the public address system outside for the food mission. The people at Wamba were given three days' worth of food, and this resulted in a lot of dancing. I also remember a young African woman who was very thin and who had traveled a long way to get to Wamba. As we were closing the doors on an empty truck, she had tears streaming down her face, and she pleaded with us to give her something, anything to eat. We had given the church a couple of 90-kilogram bags, and so we were able to help her from those bags.

UGANDA

This time I was invited by Bishop Aswa Isaac to come to Uganda in 2008. Northern Uganda was finally at peace because of an agreement between the Uganda government and the Lord's Resistance Army. For 20 years the Lord's Resistance Army, with their abducted children soldiers, controlled much of the north and terrorized villagers with automatic weapons and machetes. With the war just over, the problems that they faced in the north included a drought, which affected the crop production, sky-high food prices, and a withdrawal of food relief agencies. Because the war was over, non-government agencies were redirecting their efforts to other hot spots like the Sudan and the Democratic Republic of the Congo. We picked up Don at the Entebbe Airport and made our preparations to buy food, get a truck, and head north to Lira and beyond.

In an area called Adwari, we were able to give out a week's worth of maize and beans to a few hundred hungry poor who were mostly Christian already. While the adults were lining up for food, the African driver named Simon and I were making peanut butter sandwiches on the hood of a car for the crowd of poorly clothed children. At one point, I looked up and saw what appeared to be a ten-year-old boy who had an open sore on his chest about the size of a shirt button. I called the boy over and found in my bag a large box of Band-Aids and a tube of Neosporin antibiotic cream. When I finished dressing his sore, I found myself surrounded by the medical needs of at least 50 children. For the next hour I watched them one by one point to bleeding cuts and open sores. It wasn't until about ten minutes into this spontaneous children's Band-Aid clinic that it occurred to me that I was working with blood. I shot up a quick prayer and asked the Lord to protect me from the AIDS virus.

The next food distribution area was farther north, and we drove on foot paths to the village of Bolonyo. In 2004, the Lord's Resistance Army had come there to pillage, rape, and murder these precious village people. At Bolonyo, 385 men, women, and children who had been gunned down by the LRA were buried in mass graves that were covered with cement. These people were traumatized by a horrific tragedy, and this horseshoe-shaped mass grave was an ever-present memorial to the atrocities they went through in 2004. Over 2,000 people came out for our food distribution, and if poverty could be measured in degrees, then these people appeared to be even poorer and in more need of food than the previous village. I saw the typical signs of malnutrition and a dog that was a walking skeleton. They sat under the grove trees and waited for Don to start.

> *These people were traumatized by a horrific tragedy, and this horseshoe-shaped mass grave was an ever-present memorial to the atrocities they went through in 2004.*

When Don preached, he told them how valuable and important they were to God and that God had not abandoned them. When he gave an invitation to receive Christ as their Lord and Savior, dozens came forward and got on their knees to pray. Bishop Isaac told me that he had sent a pastor up there to start a new church from those who had come forward from Don's invitation.

WANTED: CHRISTIANS READY FOR THE MASTER'S USE

The Bible teaches that God places a great value on that one Christian who loves to be committed and will not compromise his or her walk or talk. It's as if God is searching for useful Christians and He looks down at you, sees your faithfulness, and says, "I can use this son; I can use this daughter, for My special assignments." Listen to what Paul tells Timothy:

> *But in a great house there are not only vessels of gold and silver but also of wood and clay, some for honor and some for dishonor. Therefore if anyone cleanses himself from the latter, he will be a vessel for honor, sanctified and useful for the Master, prepared for every good work* (2 Timothy 2:20-21).

Preparation for a life of usefulness is a partnership between you and God. You provide the faithfulness to follow His Word, and He will provide everything else. You show the Lord consistency and commitment, and in time He will give you a calling, specific assignments, and a purpose for living that will give you greater joy than you ever thought imaginable.

Points to Ponder

1. The trips that the author made to Africa combined food and clothes distribution with preaching the message of Christ's love and His work on the cross. Why is combining the distribution of food to the hungry and preaching the Gospel a better approach than just distributing food?

_____

_____

_____

_____

_____

2. Can you think of any times in the Bible where preaching and feeding the crowds were combined?

_____

_____

_____

_____

_____

3. What are some of the great needs around the world? Write them down. How might you be a solution to those needs?

_____

_____

_____

_____

_____

4. According to Second Timothy 2:20-21, how can we be better prepared to be vessels of honor, useful to the master, and prepared for every good work?

_____

_____

_____

_____

_____

Chapter 14

HURRICANE KATRINA

In the late summer of 2005, almost everyone found themselves glued to their television sets because of the devastation caused by Hurricane Katrina. As the news unfolded, it proved to be the most destructive and costliest hurricane in the history of the United States. Hurricane Katrina did $81.2 billion in damage, knocked out the electricity of three million people, and caused 1,836 deaths in just a few days after it slammed into Louisiana, Mississippi, and Alabama.

Hurricane Katrina did $81.2 billion in damage, knocked out the electricity of three million people, and caused 1,836 deaths in just a few days after it slammed into Louisiana, Mississippi, and Alabama.

I found myself with about 20 or more other pastors in the Lehigh Valley area, and we were discussing what we could do to help. Pastor Gary Kantola of Our Father's House said that he had learned from a pastor friend in Alabama that Biloxi and Gulfport had been severely hit, and that areas north of there had not been reached by the American Red Cross, the Salvation Army, or even FEMA.

At the same time, my wife, who works for a yearbook publisher, was meeting with the principal from one of her accounts, which happened to be a Seventh Day Adventist school. Nancy and the principal were discussing my recent missions trip to Africa when he commented that a group of his students were also going down to Mississippi on a local missions trip. They apparently had a sister school down there that was being used as a hub for food distribution. He went on to say how he had spoken to the principal of that school and found out that many parts of Mississippi had been devastated by the hurricane but the media had been focusing all their attention on New Orleans.

Because of this, many parts of Mississippi were being neglected by the bigger relief agencies. When I heard this and coupled it with what I had heard from Gary Kantola, God's direction was becoming clear. When it comes to questions like where or when, the Lord will often reinforce a confirmation from more than one source. That Thursday morning a plan was put in motion to pool together our church resources and send food and supplies using Bread of Life International. I volunteered to spearhead the effort, and once again, I felt like God was using me for His purposes.

But where do you begin? Mississippi is a big state. I spent a few minutes praying about where to go and then sat down at the computer and Googled "churches in Mississippi." After getting the phone numbers, I printed a map of Mississippi and systematically worked the phones, starting with churches and pastors on the Gulf coast. Well, it didn't take many calls to realize that the phones were out and so were the cell phone towers. I kept working my way north from the Gulf until I made a connection. Finally, the phone rang at the Central Baptist Church in Hattiesburg, Mississippi, and I was able to speak with a Rev. Ray Joslyn. He confirmed to me that the phones in the center of the state had just been restored and that the phones were completely out in southern Mississippi. He told me that his church was collecting donations of food and that a distribution center had been set up in the church's gym. His gym was full, and supplies were not in short supply, so Ray suggested that we go to Liberty Assembly of God in Gautier, Mississippi, which was right on the Gulf, where the destruction was the greatest. I kept trying to get through, and after a couple of days, I finally connected with a worker at the church.

Meanwhile, the *Morning Call*, a local newspaper, did an article on how pastors and churches in the Lehigh Valley were mobilizing to take food relief and other supplies down to the Mississippi Gulf. The paper mentioned that while the media had been largely focused on Louisiana, equally hard-hit Mississippi was not getting the same television coverage or the same attention for hurricane relief. But the churches in the Allentown, Bethlehem, and Easton area had mobilized and were taking food donations to the lesser-known Katrina-ravaged areas of the Mississippi Gulf.

Even the local American Red Cross began directing people with bags of donations to give them to the Bread of Life International drop-off station. Pastor Gary Kantola and his board at Our Father's House had allowed their church building to be turned into one big warehouse. The sanctuary and certain rooms were off-limits, but the hall, the foyer, and the fellowship room were packed with canned food, dry foods, baby formula, paper towels, and cleaning supplies that were stacked three- to five-feet high. Supplies were everywhere! On the day of departure, there was no shortage of volunteers for packing the truck, and we were on the road by nine that morning. Other volunteers for making the relief trip to Mississippi included people from my church, Living Word, as well as volunteers from Resurrection Worship, which included their pastor, Jay Maldonado. We were a convoy consisting of one big truck and a large passenger van full of people who had taken time off from their jobs in order to deliver the goods.

Heading for the Gulf Coast from Pennsylvania during that time in history was an experience in itself. People were so friendly and helpful, especially when they discovered that we were on a mission to help Katrina victims. Hotels were giving discounts or even free rooms to those who were on their way to the Gulf. An Auto Zone in Tennessee gave us free truck wipers when our wipers broke down and thanked us for all that we were doing to help fellow Americans in the disaster area. We would stop to eat and notice other church vans and trucks headed for the Gulf, and on the highways in Alabama it seemed like half of the traffic consisted of church vans and trucks carrying roofing supplies, wood frames, and dry wall. We even saw a large flatbed truck carrying about 20 large outdoor shower units. It felt like a happening, and we were on a special mission. Getting close to the coast, we could see trees down, gas stations full of twisted metal, and motel roofs torn off. It was a little bit eerie to see the aftermath of such a powerful hurricane.

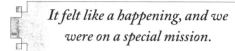

It felt like a happening, and we were on a special mission.

When we got to Gautier, Mississippi, we found Liberty Assembly of God and immediately pulled in and greeted those in charge of the fellowship hall, which was now a depleted distribution center. Listen to how God worked His plan.

This church was just a few blocks from the Gulf of Mexico, and they were helping hurricane victims by the hundreds. The week before, a tractor trailer had come from a church in the north to Liberty Assembly of God without one person calling them in or pleading for help. Liberty had turned their fellowship hall into a hurricane relief hub with food, hygiene products, and cleaning supplies for Katrina victims. When our truck had arrived in Gautier, the church's supplies were extremely low, and the tables that had been stacked to the ceiling with cereal, peanut butter, canned goods, diapers, toiletries, clothes, and detergent were now down to practically nothing. So with almost zero communication and without any human coordination, we arrived with over $12,000 in supplies from eastern Pennsylvania and restocked everything in that fellowship hall, and did it in a place where the need was extreme.

LOVE NEEDS TO BECOME ACTION

God always backs up His statements of love with actions

of love, kindness, and good works. During Jesus' three years of ministry, the Bible tells us, *"God anointed Jesus of Nazareth with the Holy Spirit and with power, who went about doing good and healing all who were oppressed..."* (Acts 10:38). We are supposed to be imitators of Christ, and so we need to ask Him for opportunities and "go about doing good." The good works we do can never be our payment for a pass into Heaven. We believe, we receive salvation as a free gift, and then we do goods works, not the other way around.

For by grace you have been saved through faith, and that not of yourselves; it is the gift of God, not of works, lest anyone should boast. For we are His workmanship, created in Christ Jesus for good works, which God prepared beforehand that we should walk in them (Ephesians 2:8-10).

Christ-like love will always express itself in actions and good works.

Jesus taught this in His story of the Good Samaritan. What I love about this story is that it shows not only that actions speak louder than religiosity, but also that doing good to someone is not conditional on the person's worth but should always spring into action when there is a pressing human need.

But he (a certain lawyer), wanting to justify himself, said to Jesus, "And who is my neighbor?"

Then Jesus answered and said: "A certain man went down from Jerusalem to Jericho, and fell among thieves, who stripped him of his clothing, wounded him, and departed, leaving him half dead. Now by chance a certain priest came down that road. And when he saw him, he passed by on the other side. Likewise a Levite, when he arrived at the place, came and looked, and passed by on the other side. But a certain Samaritan, as he journeyed, came where he was. And when he saw him, he had compassion. So he went to him and bandaged his wounds, pouring on oil and wine; and he set him on his own animal, brought him to an inn, and took care of him. On the next day, when he departed, he took out two denarii, gave them to the innkeeper, and said to him, 'Take care of him; and whatever more you spend, when I come again, I will repay you.' So which of these three do you think was neighbor to him who fell among the thieves?' And he said, "He who showed mercy on him." Then Jesus said to him, "Go and do likewise" (Luke 10:29-37).

An entire book could be written on this passage, but for the purposes of this chapter, Luke 10:29-37 is about Jesus teaching His listeners a life application—that love needs to be an action. It's not enough to appear religious and not lift a finger to help; there needs to be compassion toward our neighbor. Taking constructive action is the fulfillment to love the Lord our God with all our heart and to love our neighbor as ourselves. Who is my neighbor? Anyone left bleeding, cold, or hungry. If people are sheep, then God wants us to become shepherds. We're supposed to be the good guys!

Points to Ponder

1. How did the author get confirmation as to where to go in the hurricane hit areas of the Gulf?

_____

_____

_____

2. When you see a need in your church or community, what early steps can you take to help?

_____

_____

_____

3. What are some reasons why people might hesitate to help out in a crisis?

_____

_____

_____

4. Read again the story of the Good Samaritan in Luke 10:29-37. Can you retell the story in a contemporary setting? Why did the Good Samaritan choose to help his neighbor?

_____

_____

_____

Chapter 15

INTIMACY TRUMPS MINISTRY

In Chapter 7, I shared about a time of preparation. For me, this was a time when, ministry-wise, I was a nobody, a peon who was in charge of nothing. During this period, the Lord taught me how incredibly important it was to be close to Him every day. Intimacy trumps ministry. Even though I had no ministry or special calling, I was strongly impressed to spend chunks of time in sweet communion, deep worship, and personal interaction by praying. I would worship with my first cup of coffee and then look for opportunities to get with Him throughout the day.

Intimacy trumps ministry. Even though I had no ministry or special calling, I was strongly impressed to spend chunks of time in sweet communion, deep worship, and personal interaction by praying.

I remember one time when my wife asked if I would clean out our big, old two-car garage. I started to put some boxes away, and while I was cleaning, I kept singing to the Lord. Just like that, two hours of praise and worship went by and it felt like time had stood still. I had to explain to Nancy why I didn't get more done that Saturday afternoon!

This period in my life was also a time when I had developed a voracious appetite for the Bible. Without a ministry, Jesus was my only calling. He taught me that this is my primary calling and that although a ministry call can develop, God's call to have me close is laying the foundation for any usefulness later on. He was teaching me to implement the instructions that Jesus gave to the Church of Ephesus in Revelation:

> *I know your works...and have labored for My names sake and have not become weary. Never the less I have this against you, that you have left your first love* (Revelation 2:2-4).

Jesus was putting closeness over and above ministry. This period in my life taught me that if ministry—that is, the work of shepherding—were to somehow disappear for a while, I cannot let anything or anyone shake me from my close relationship with Jesus Christ. He needs to be my everything, and by God's grace, ministry will never make me too busy to spend time in close communion with the Lord. That's my first call.

Two Calls

Making the transition from sheep to shepherd is a process that involves two calls from God. The first call is to become a following sheep of Jesus Christ. Here we get to experience His love and come to know His voice. The moment we believe that Jesus died on the cross for our sins and ask Him to be the Lord, we are His. But the second call of God is an invitation to be a shepherd. As stated before, shepherding sheep can involve a wide range of gifts and ministries.

Paul and Peter both had two callings. In Acts 9, Paul saw a heavenly light, fell to the ground, and had an encounter with the resurrected Jesus. This was Paul's conversion call, and the call to be an apostle came after conversion. Paul opens his letter to the Romans by identifying himself with both callings. *Paul, a bond servant of Jesus Christ, called to be an apostle* (Rom. 1:1).

Peter also writes a similar introduction in his second letter and identifies himself using two callings. In Second Peter 1:1, he writes, *"Simon Peter, a bond servant and apostle of Jesus Christ."* With both Paul and Peter, they identify themselves as called to be a bondservant of Jesus Christ first and apostle second.

As I ponder these callings, I can see the divine wisdom in waiting and preparing sheep before making them shepherds. When I came back to the Lord in 1996, I was a found sheep, but I wasn't ready to shepherd. In 1997, it was as if I was in the school of the Holy Spirit for a couple of years. God's number one priority was to lay down for me the foundation of having a close daily relationship with Jesus. He could call me into ministry later on or He could put me on the shelf for a while. That's the Lord's prerogative. But whether He uses me or not, my first calling is to be a sheep and a servant of Jesus Christ. Getting the second call to be a shepherd for others is a promotion and a privilege. It's rich icing on an already great cake.

CONCLUSION

Every Christian's life is like a journey. But what kind of journey will your Christian life be? You can let the years fly by and do nothing of eternal significance, or you can become useful to the leadings of the Holy Spirit. He longs to have you busy with His work—a vessel of honor, fit for the Master's use. That can be you!

After having read this book, I hope that you will be driven to do three things; first, assess yourself; second, ask the Lord to help you to get ready for service; and finally, pray that He will call on you to pick up the tools of a shepherd and begin to shepherd others. There are literally billions who need to hear the good news of Jesus Christ. There is a significant shortage of "called" pastors and teachers. Parts of Africa are on fire with famine, war, and the AIDS pandemic. All over the world orphans need homes, children need role models, and people everywhere need good shepherds who can demonstrate the love of Jesus and lead others to be salt and light in the world.

Assess your situation by first asking yourself, how much time do I have left? In other words, how old are you, and what's left in front of you? That's how much time you have left to make your life count for the Kingdom of God. After I had squandered my late twenties and all of my thirties, I stood at a crossroads and looked at my future. The Lord began to burn a passage in my heart, and it was Psalm 90:12: *Teach us to number our days aright, that we may gain a heart of wisdom* .

I began to wish that I hadn't wasted so many years. I did not want my life to be just about over before I turned around and started loving the Lord back. One daytime television soap got it right when it said, "Like sands through the hourglass, so are the days of our lives." Every day we get from the Lord is precious and has the potential to bless others.

The next thing I would assess would be natural talents, learning, and gifts. Romans 12:6 says that we all have different gifts. It could be teaching, encouraging others, contributing to the physical needs of others, doing acts of mercy, leading worship, shepherding a congregation, or building up others with a prophetic and timely word. In First Corinthians 12, Paul gives us a long list of spiritual gifts, and all of them are designed to help and bless others.

After you've assessed yourself and your situation, begin to ask the Lord to help you get ready for when He calls you. Make sure that your Bible time and prayer time is habitual. Get serious about living for God and radical in your commitment to following Jesus.

Finally, seek the Lord every day and pray that He will call you into His service. Ask for it and pray big. What's impossible with God? At this writing, I am asking the Lord for enough money to build a multi-functional community campus and orphanage for Malawi. Pray big and have faith! Nothing is more exciting than the privilege of being called by God to do His work and going from sheep to shepherd. And as you stay close to the Lord and remain faithful to Him, don't be surprised if you hear Him someday whisper to your heart, "Do you love me?...Feed My sheep."

Points to Ponder

1. Why does intimacy with God trump ministry? How does a close walk with the Lord lay the foundation for a life of service to others?

_____

_____

_____

2. Explain the two callings of God. Can you have the first calling but not the second one? Why?

_____

_____

_____

3. According to Psalm 90:12, what should we be numbering and why? How much time do you think you have left to live for God?

_____

_____

_____

4. What has the Holy Spirit been putting on your heart? What great things would you like to accomplish in service to Christ?

_____

_____

_____

5. Are you ready for the call to serve others? Will you ask the Lord of the harvest to send you as a worker in His fields?

_____

_____

_____

REFERENCES

Paula Simmons and Carol Ekarius, *Storey's Guide to Raising Sheep* (North Adams, Massachusetts: Storey Publishing, 2001).

Chuck Wooster, *Living With Sheep* (Guilford, Connecticut: The Lyon Press, 2005).

ABOUT RICK TUNIS

For more information or to contact the author for speaking engagements:

RICK TUNIS MINISTRIES
P.O. BOX 3237
BETHLEHEM, PA 18017
1-866-333 9815
EMAIL: RICKTUNIS@YMAIL.COM
WWW.RICKTUNIS.COM | WWW.BREADOFLIFEINTL.NET

If you would like to make a donation to Bread of Life International you can mail it to the address listed above.